XPORT (France). -year-old aluminium . 57ft overall and has d transatlantic and -Rio races. Design re Mauric. Co-skippered uillet and J. P. Millet. ıp 5.520 days.

BURTON CUTTER (Britain). Newly-built 80ft aluminium ketch, design, John Sharp, sponsor, Burton and International Wool Secretariat. Skipper, Leslie Williams who won last two-man Round Britain race and 1971 Capetown-Rio. H'cap 0.8543 days.

CSeRB (Italy). 50ft glass fibre ketch designed Robert Clark with facility for crew to sail her from below under Dio Malingri de Bagnolo, experienced ocean racer. H'cap 7.798 days.

COPERNICUS (Poland). 45ft mahogany ketch built 1973. Design, Liskiewicz. Skipper, Zygfryd Perlicki of Yacht Club Staczni Gdanskeij, who own her. H'cap 9.336 days.

ADVENTURE (Britain). Royal Navy entry sailing to Capetown under Patrick Bryans. Nicholson glass fibre 55 footer. Skippered in turn Malcolm Skene (Capetown-Sydney), George Vallings (Sydney-Rio de Janeiro) and Roy Mullender (Rio-Portsmouth). H'cap 6.743 days.

TAURANGA (Italy). Mixed crew of French, Swiss and Italian under Erik Pascoli. Glass fibre 55 ft yawl of Sparkman and Stephens design. H'cap 7.113 days.

PETER VON DANZIG (Germany). Pre-war 59ft Bermuda yawl. Designed Henrey Gruber, 1936. Skippered Achim Meyer and Reinhard Laucht, and crewed from Kiel Marine Academy. H'cap 6.174 days.

GRAND LOUIS (France). Owned by Andre Viant and crewed by relatives. Glass fibre schooner, 61ft. Designed Dominique Preles, built 1973. H'cap 5.45 days.

PEN 74ft speci Andr Eric T French naval crew living in spartan conditions. H'cap 1.339 days.

Theirs is the glory

By the same author

THE IMPOSSIBLE VOYAGE

Theirs is the glory

by

CHAY BLYTH

HODDER AND STOUGHTON

LONDON SYDNEY AUCKLAND TORONTO

 ISBN 0 340 18518 X. *Printed in Great Britain for Hodder and Stroughton Limited, St. Paul's House, Warwick Lane, London Ec4P 4AH by Thomson Litho Ltd., East Kilbride, Scotland.*

To "Union Jack" Hayward

Author's note

This is the part of the book that I personally dread. It is the 'thank you' bit and the danger is that you always miss someone out. Also, if I expressed my sincere gratitude to everyone who helped with the *Great Britain II* project, I would have no room for the story.

Nevertheless, there are people who have given much more than work and money towards the success of our voyage and whom I want to thank publicly and permanently. My wife, Maureen, and my daughter, Samantha, made sacrifices I cannot begin to describe. Jack Hayward, the main sponsor, is a unique person, totally beyond my understanding; an amazing and generous man who defies convention and must surely qualify for the title of the happiest millionaire. Friends like Chris Waddington, John Wright, David Strong and Frank Allen all gave their best and helped me to overcome many obstacles. Firms, large and small, who gave products and expertise have proved that British industry still has heart.

The phrase 'without whom this book would not have been written' belongs to my friend of long standing, Terry Bond, who edited the logs and helped to put the full stops in the right places. A slice of praise must go too to Winifred Powis who managed to transcribe my scrawley logs and Anne Pocklington who corrected the spelling mistakes.

But the biggest thanks of all must go to the Parachute Brigade and the men who make up the 16th Regiment. Everyone, from the Brigadier to the newest recruit, supported us with enthusiasm and practical advice and help. And, of course, they produced a great crew.

CHAY BLYTH

Contents

Colour illustrations

between page 112 and 113

Acknowledgements

[1] *The Illustrated London News*
[2] Alec Honey

Black and white illustrations

Arrival at Sydney[1]
A Christmas barbecue in Sydney
The new mizzen mast being prepared
Pete and Robbie servicing the winches
Number 4 loose luffed and boomed out
Eric admires the view in Rio
The keel at Rio, showing the leak
Len, painting the deck at Rio
At the finishing line, Portsmouth[4]
The trophies won by *Great Britain II*

Acknowledgements

[1] Peter Bates
[2] *The Sunday Times*
[3] Alec Honey
[4] Beken of Cowes

PART ONE

The End—and the Beginning

I

SAILING BY MYSELF WESTWARDS AROUND THE WORLD WAS an interesting experience. The actual sailing was exhilarating, exciting, sometimes frightening and occasionally boring. I was exhilarated at the start of the voyage when I had left all the ballyhoo behind me and I knew that I was attempting what no man had ever done before, and I looked forward to the battle. I was excited as the voyage progressed and I came to realise just what a magnificent boat *British Steel* was, and how compatible we really were. I had my first taste of fear in the Indian Ocean. As with all unpleasant experiences, it tends to fade in the memory. However, as I read my logs for that day, April 29th, 1971, the feelings flood back. I wrote:

> 14.15. Everywhere is white, the spray gets knocked off the waves with such ferocity. I was going to try to take some photographs but it's ludicrous.
>
> The Atlantic was never like this. The waves follow

> one after the other like legions going into battle. The discipline is rigid, as one wave goes down another rises to take its place.
>
> If ever I dream, I'll dream of this storm. The hurricanes in the Atlantic never haunted me but this one could. I just close my eyes and see those white-blue legions rising and falling but always advancing.
>
> My heart goes out to the men at Dartmouth at Philip's yard [the builders of *British Steel*]. It would only have taken one of them to have shirked his job, and the sea would find the weak spot, and then it would work on it until it got us.
>
> Stay strong, *British Steel.* You have my life in your hands now. There is nothing I can do. It's up to you and our Lord.
>
> For the first time in my life I've been honestly and genuinely frightened. It's always been a kind of curiosity. But here and now I'll say, without any embarrassment, I am frightened.

Maybe reading that in cold print it sounds a bit melodramatic. But I would not change a word because I remember how it was written, not with a typewriter and virgin white paper, in a warm home with my family around me, but in a damp log book with a pencil that was difficult to decipher afterwards. I was battened down and being tossed around the cabin like a pea in a referee's whistle. *British Steel* was a piece of flotsam in a very angry sea. I was frightened and those few sentences were offered more as a prayer than anything else.

Fortunately life on board a big yacht by yourself is not all like that. The times that generate real emotions are few and far between and although I have a mental discipline that keeps me busy for as long as possible there are inevitable periods when boredom can set in. So when I had read the few books I took with me—everything from romances to *Teach Yourself Navigation*—I avoided sloth by asking a lot of questions and studying humanity in some depth. That was great, but the only person around to answer the questions, and the only example of humanity on board, was me. Inevitably then I took a long look at Chay Blyth.

I am not sure that I particularly liked what I discovered. For example, I soon realised that I am a selfish man who will declare undying love for his wife and family with one breath and with the next up-and-away for ten months of peril on the high seas. A considerate man mindful of his responsibilities would not do such a thing. Nevertheless, I have a deep love for my wife Maureen and my daughter Samantha and I am not afraid to declare it. My yearning for experience and adventure is tempered by my love for them and it is because of them that I calculate every action and assess every risk.

I was rather surprised to find that Chay Blyth can also be a moody man, depressed when things are going wrong and elated by the slightest upturn in fortunes. Other items on the debit side are that the subject has a temper which needs controlling and that he suffers fools badly. On a brighter note, he is determined, physically fit, honest, and will listen to advice and assess it carefully before making his own irrevocable decision. (That is my opinion of Chay Blyth. Further on in this book, you will see that a psychiatrist's opinion is rather different!)

It is honestly difficult to say how that lone voyage changed me, but I do know that it gave me a revised view of the importance of life. Money, houses, cars, eating out, drinking, dancing, seeking more possessions—all these things have become a comfortable part of our daily life. Individually they are harmless, yet collectively they are eroding real life. People, ecology, environment, nature—these are the important things. I came back to the Hamble in the Autumn of 1971 determined to put second the man-made pleasures and to lead a more fulfilled life. I also made a private promise to myself that I would try hard to put adventure behind me and be satisfied with my achievements to date.

After all, my lot was quite a happy one. At the end of the voyage, I was offered and accepted a pleasant and worthwhile job with the Outward Bound Trust. Lecturing on my experiences produced a very reasonable income and my book *The Impossible Voyage* was selling well throughout the world. I had a large bungalow standing quietly in its own grounds in Newbury, Berkshire. I had a great wife and a super daughter. And I was nagged by an ache that just would not go away. I knew about the Round-the-World Race and more than anything else I wanted to be part of it, to enter and to win.

Even before the voyage of *British Steel* I had heard about the race, then just the germ of an idea. It was being nurtured by two well known figures in the sailing world, Anthony Churchill and Guy Pearse. Anthony was then publisher of *Yachting and Boating Weekly* and had been navigator on *Morning Cloud* in the Sydney-Hobart Race. He had also navigated *Lutine* in the Bermuda Race and *Phantom* in the Fastnet. He was a regular member of Ted Heath's crew on the new *Morning Cloud.* Guy Pearse had been responsible for organising the *Observer* Single-handed Transatlantic Race and the *Daily Express* Round Britain Race. He was a keen sailor and had once navigated a whale catcher in the Antarctic.

Here then were two talented and experienced yachtsmen with a good idea and the drive to get it off the ground. They started off on the right foot by producing a four page brochure outlining their plans.

> An international round the world race for fully crewed ocean racers with maximum seventy-three feet overall [said the brochure]. A Race round the World for large ocean racers is provisionally planned for September 1973. The race will start from Plymouth about two weeks after the end of Fastnet and there will be compulsory stops at Cape Town, Sydney, and Rio de Janeiro. The race will finish at Plymouth and is expected to last six months. Entries will only be accepted

> for fully crewed Class 1 yachts rated under the IOR Rule. The maximum overall length allowed is 73 feet, the maximum rating is 70 feet, and the minimum rating is 33 feet. This race would have been hard to organise while there was a multiplicity of national rules. Now there is one International rule and one set of international safety rules is coming into force.
>
> The September 1973 date is chosen with care; it will give owners enough time to prepare and equip their entries. The race starts after the RORC season is over to give overseas visitors to the UK circuit a chance to race all or part of the way home. The timing will also allow yachts to round Cape Horn in reasonable weather.

Considering that the race was then in embryo, Anthony and Guy were surprisingly close to what eventually were the final arrangements. This soothsaying went even further for under the heading, "Entries" they wrote:

> A minimum of a dozen entries seems likely. Yachtsmen of two types seem interested. First there are the ocean racers wishing a change from the shortness of today's classic races—a 73 foot yacht may travel for a month to get to a race which lasts only four days. Second are the famous "loners" who sail the oceans. Both types are attracted by a race bearing the mantle of the Old Clipper Ship contests, a race which combines tight organisation plus the spice of adventure, a race which tests equipment, seamanship and stamina to their limits. This is the race of a lifetime.

The brochure went on about the rules and the size of yachts and communications and ports of call and the dozens of aspects of such a great race. As I read it I dreamed of competing against the best in the world, men like Chichester, Knox Johnston, Tabarly and Colas. As it turned out, of course, only one of these great sailors, Eric Tabarly of France, competed in the race and the ill-luck that dogged him was one of the saddest features of the whole event. And although anyone can dream, I could not really afford the luxury of doing so because I was still busily preparing for my solo voyage. Therefore, after the initial flush of enthusiasm and gossip that is bound to accompany the announcement of such a race I pushed it to the back of my mind.

It was to be brought again into my thoughts with a real jolt when I was three-quarters of the way round the world. I received a telegram from General (now Field Marshal) Sir Michael Carver, G.C.B., C.B.E., D.S.O., M.C., A.D.C. asking if I would loan *British Steel* to the British Army for them to enter a crew in the Round-the-World Yacht Race. Obviously things were progressing from the talking stage and it did not take me long to agree to the Army's request. I had enjoyed my time as a soldier and Her Majesty's Forces had been good to me. I had learned a lot from them and they had looked after me and moulded me. I felt that lending *British Steel* was one way for me to say a sort of "thank you" to the Army.

That may sound a bit twee so I should explain that the Army is not all good. In fact there is a lot of bad in the forces, as there is bound to be in any big organisation. You have to look at it objectively, appreciate the good points and put up with the bad ones. So far as I am concerned the Army gave me an interesting life and just like the recruiting posters say it was full of excitement and opportunity. As I mentioned earlier one tends to forget the more unpleasant parts of the past.

There was another consideration when I decided how to reply to the General's request. Big boats such as *British Steel, Sir Thomas Lipton,* and *Gypsy Moth* were designed as single handed craft. This meant that only one person at a time was getting real pleasure out of them and to my mind that is all wrong. Boats are to sail and when they are not being used for racing they should be used for relaxing. It makes me mad to think that a yacht like *Gypsy Moth,* a beautiful craft that has achieved world recognition, should be stuck in concrete when it could have given so much more joy on the sea. Just to watch a yacht like that sailing evokes in me an emotional state that some people get from good music or fine writing. Sure, stick it in concrete when its life is finished, but there were years of pleasure left in Chichester's boat. To mummify it was criminal.

How different is the story of that equally famous yacht, *Sir Thomas Lipton*. Hundreds of young men and women have thrilled to sailing in her and she has become a legend in her own time. Shortly after I returned to Britain I had a roundabout request from an American maritime museum who wanted to buy *British Steel* and financially it was well worth considering. Quite honestly if I had accepted I would not have been able to sleep nights. To stick a boat in concrete is like confining people to bed when they are not ill.

My radioed reply to the General read: "Delighted to loan *British Steel* to the Army. Look forward to meeting you to discuss details."

* * *

The months after my return to the Hamble went by in a whirl. Naturally I was personally proud of my achievement but I was amazed at the interest it generated. Suddenly from being "the sergeant that rowed the Atlantic with Captain John Ridgway," I was Chay Blyth the man who sailed round the world the wrong way. I learned long ago that the only way to stay sane when newspapers, magazines, and the telly start on you is never ever to believe your own publicity. So while it was very nice to be invited here, there and everywhere, and hear adjectives like heroic bandied about whenever someone introduced me as a speaker, I took it all with a pinch of salt. I believe anyone can be a hero, but to be a live hero is best. My formula was simple—careful planning, attention to detail, hard work, the right tools for the job, and a big slice of help from Up Above. That's what got me and *British Steel* through and the same requirements would be applied to all my future ventures.

As well as the speaking engagements (at one time they averaged four a week both in Britain and Europe) I was making personal appearances, guesting on television "chat" shows, doing radio record programmes, dashing about the world for Outward Bound, honouring my commitments to the British Steel Corporation, visiting the world's boat shows, opening exhibitions, making my right arm limp at book signing sessions, writing newspaper and magazine articles, getting fat again and generally reflecting in the odd moments that I stopped for a breather that it is a mad, mad, mad, mad world.

After four months of land living again I was almost at the end of my tether and decided that it was time for Maureen and me to take a wee holiday. Frank Allen, a Southampton businessman who had helped me so much with the circumnavigation, had some flats out in the Bahamas and suggested that we join him and his wife Audrey for a holiday out there.

Unfortunately the dates Frank suggested did not coincide precisely with the times I could manage. The arrangements were all made in a bit of a rush and when we caught the plane we were not quite sure what we were letting ourselves in for. It had been arranged that we would be met, but as we touched down in Freeport, Maureen wondered aloud what would happen if there was no one to meet us.

"We'll leave the airport, find the nearest hotel, stay in it until our money runs out and then use our return tickets to fly home," I said, always one for the simple solution. I was to discover that it would not have been the ideal answer because at Bahamian prices we could have afforded to stay in the country for about 48 hours.

However, we need not have worried. As we walked down the steps from the aircraft I looked across the tarmac and could hardly believe my eyes. There, in neon lights about twenty feet high, I read, "GRAND BAHAMAS WELCOMES YACHTSMAN CHAY BLYTH".

The great and gaudy sign had been arranged by two friends of Frank's who had been asked to meet us. They were

Betty and Joe McConville who live out in Freeport, and two finer characters I have yet to meet. The man who coined the phrase "all go" must have been watching Betty at the time because she has a vigour that is insatiable. As befits her copper hair she can be fiery when necessary and it is a brave person who will say "no" if Betty says "yes". Small wonder then that within seconds of clearing customs at Freeport, without a chance even to wash or change after our six hour flight, we were in the back of Joe's car being whisked to our first encounter with the Bahamian party scene.

I understand that now Mr. Pinling and his new regime have taken over the Bahamas things have changed drastically and the expatriate British community has virtually disappeared from the islands. But at that time the coloured takeover was nothing more than a dark cloud on the horizon and the parties, very large and very Bohemian, came fast and furious.

It was at this initial party with Betty and Joe that I first met Jack Hayward. The name rang a mental bell and I wondered if it could be the man made famous by two tremendous gestures, the acquisition of Lundy Island and its presentation to Great Britain, and the financing of the return of that most magnificent of all iron ships, the SS *Great Britain* from the Falklands to Bristol. My new acquaintance was indeed the same J. Hayward, Esq., O.B.E., and as the party swung on its inevitably merry way I found myself thinking about the motivations of the man.

I find it fascinating that anyone should choose to make philanthropic gestures in such unusual and interesting ways. It is easy to give away surplus cash to worthwhile charities and one is often praised and honoured for doing so. But here was a man who sought glory not for himself but for his country. He had earned himself the nickname of "Union Jack" Hayward because of his fierce patriotism and his anxiety to preserve all things British.

Unfortunately I did not get more than two or three minutes to chat with him at this first meeting, because he was obviously a tremendously popular chap, and our conversation was punctuated by a series of casual interruptions from his friends. So while he chatted to them I slunk quietly into a corner and continued to stuff myself with champagne and caviar. Poor old Chay!

Altogether I spent fourteen days in the Bahamas and on most of them, it seemed, I would bump into Jack Hayward and his charming wife Jean. I gave a lecture to the local Rotary Club and Jack proposed the vote of thanks. I talked after dinner to the local sailing club and who should stand up to say ta very much? Jack Hayward. I gave another talk to another club and there was no need for me to ask who was making the response. Those readers who heard my lecture more than once after the solo voyage, will know that although I vary it slightly according to the audience, it contains basically the same stories and the same jokes, so that it is a tribute to Jack's staying power that he managed to sound convincing as he gave one reply after another.

Eventually, I suppose working on the principle that if you can't beat them join them, he invited Maureen and me up to his house. It was a beautiful home—and I do mean home. Not at all ostentatious; it was a spacious and comfortable residence with its own swimming pool and an atmosphere that told you that pleasant folk lived there. I have a theory that happy homes have a feeling all of their own, and it does not matter whether it is a council house or a castle. I have a morbid fear of settling down but if I ever do (and even that admission of the possibility will make Maureen whoop for joy), I would like a place similar to Jack's pad in the Bahamas. Although he now lives for most of the year on his dairy farm in Sussex, I believe he still keeps his Bahamas home, and having seen it I envy him.

At the cocktail session at Jack's house I met his three children. Actually "children" is a misleading word because two of them at least are of voting age and the youngest, Jonathan, is well on the way. He was on vacation from Stowe School, a quiet and modest young man with a will very much of his own. His elder brother Rick is much more outward-going, a chip off the Hayward block and a seeker of experiences. Rick has a job with the World Wildlife Fund, which involves him in flying to many countries to drum up support for this very worthwhile cause. (Incidentally, I am told by my wife and other female friends that Rick is an extremely handsome young man, who must be a strong contender for The World's Most Eligible Bachelor title. I take their word for it.) The only daughter is Susan, a smashing blonde who was then engaged and in fact was married on the day the Whitbread Race started.

The Haywards are a most pleasant and closely knit family and I am told that before any major decision is made they all discuss it and everyone's view is taken into account.

I should explain that at this time there was absolutely no suggestion that Jack should in any way become involved in sponsoring an entry for the Round-the-World Race. I discussed my plans with him because he seemed interested and I quickly become enthusiastic if I have a receptive audience. But as far as I knew we had almost got a sponsor for a big new world-beating boat. My friend and agent, Terry Bond, had been quietly negotiating with one of the major international petrol companies; we had met the director who could say yea or nay and he had appeared keen, and so far as we knew the show was as good as on the road.

From my point of view, then, it was nothing more than a gesture of friendship when Jack and Jean came to the airport to say goodbye on the day Maureen and I left the Bahamas. His parting words: "If anything happens to your sponsor let me know. . ." were half-forgotten.

On the plane home and during the next few days Maureen and I got down to the nitty-gritty. Any wife faced with a husband like me is entitled to ask: "What the hell do you think you are doing?" Other husbands, given the choice, are at home regularly. If a fuse blows they can mend it, if the car tyre pressures need checking the chap gets down on his knees and does it. Cutting the lawn, paying the bills, moving the furniture around; when you get over the romantic bit these are the things that real husbands are all about.

Socially too the man needs to be there. The human being is a gregarious animal and parties, dances, dinners, theatre visits, trips to the coast, are usually enjoyed by the family together. Again I was asking Maureen and Samantha to make their pleasures without me. They had done it before and Maureen knew the strain it would put on them. It was no use me trotting out the cliches about the soldiers who have to serve for months abroad while their wives stay at home. Maureen had heard that before, and the obvious retort is that the soldiers do not deliberately choose to be posted. They have to follow orders.

When I sailed westwards I realised that I could never have undertaken the journey without Maureen. She had been the mainstay of the organisation, working day after day and night after night to help me with the preparations. She did jobs that no woman should be asked to do, put in hours that would make the TUC squeal with disbelief. And when she and Samantha waved me bon voyage from the Royal Southern Yacht Club, Maureen and I knew there was a very real danger we would not see each other again. For ten months Maureen lived with the fear that the phone would ring or there would be a knock on the door and she would be a widow. What made it much worse was the fact that I had deliberately chosen to risk my life in this way.

It would be silly for me to pretend that the prospect of another several months of being parted served as an injection of joy for my wife. Indeed, I would have been worried if it had!

She was entitled to state her case and although I believe I am the one who wears the trousers and makes the major decisions, I doubt whether I would have taken part in the race if Maureen had objected violently. Apart from any other consideration, her flair for getting things done is an essential part of the Blyth team. Some months before I had, with trepidation, broached the subject of the race.

"I want to enter the Round-the-World Race," I said, deciding that to plunge in would get the agony over quicker.

"I was wondering when you were going to tell me," she replied. She can be very sarcastic at times. "Chay, I know that if you want to enter that race you will enter and nothing anyone can say or do will stop you." She brushed aside my half-hearted protests and then smiled. "Actually I think it is a good idea. I am looking forward to helping."

With the ice broken and my biggest fear overcome, I was like a little boy having his first sight of the sea. Words, plans, thoughts, ideas, opinions, all came tumbling out of me literally non-stop for days.

I know that my emotions go in peaks and troughs—one of the most dangerous aspects of my character—but even that knowledge cannot abate the enthusiasm, or cure the depressions. So I deluged poor Maureen with a flood of rhetoric that would have drowned a lesser person.

First the boat. It had to be the fastest in the race, we would stretch the rules to the limit. Then the crew. All good, experienced, ocean-going men, the pick of the sailing world. The fact that we had not got a spare penny to pay for the boat, and that off-hand I could not think of one sailor who could afford the time to spend eight months at sea, were matters of detail that could be dealt with later. Anyway, the oil company had as good as promised the cash and there had to be dozens of experienced sailors clamouring to join me.

Through my days of explosive enthusiasm Maureen resignedly waited, listening always and commenting infrequently. She knew my bubble would burst as they had so often burst before, and she knew we would have to go through hell before my big dream was realised.

2

A PETROL BOMB DISRUPTED OUR DREAMS AND SHATTERED OUR illusions just a fortnight after our return from the Bahamas. It came in the form of a letter from the oil company we had counted on to provide the cash for the new boat. It seemed that we were victims of an international situation that we could do nothing about; the Arabs were becoming arrogant, oil prices were spiralling, and the oil companies were cutting down on all their commitments until the position became clearer. It was a nicely worded letter. ". . . find it difficult to turn down a proposition which basically I feel strongly about . . . sure you will have no difficulty in finding a sponsor . . . all know you have captured the imagination of everyone with your tremendous feats . . . wish you every success. . ."

So that was it. We were without a sponsor.

Luckily I am an incurable optimist in these situations because I believe we have evolved a successful formula for attracting sponsors. Or at least, I thought at that time our methods were successful, and although my faith has taken a bit of a battering since then, I will outline our approach.

It may serve as a guide to others who seek sponsorship and equally it may save a lot of wasted manhours on the parts of both the potential sponsor and sponsored.

Sponsorship is a tremendously complicated subject, which I have made my business to study. I have examined case histories and talked with people and organisations who have attracted money and those companies which have invested money. I have learned a series of facts, but sad to say they are impossible to relate to one another. There are no hard and fast rules in the game.

Big corporations and companies get dozens of letters every week from people requesting money or goods. Schweppes, Heinz, John Player, Shell, Bass Charrington, Ford, *The Times* newspapers, Hepworths—take any national name in any consumer field, and I will find you a chappie there who does little else but write nothing doing letters to those worthies who want anything from a tenner to a million for projects ranging from ballooning to the moon to giving grannie a holiday because she has not seen the sea for forty years. Now it may be that the idea is a good one and that the company concerned could benefit from supporting it. The secret is to get the initial approach so right that the benefits are immediately apparent, and inevitably you move on to the next stage of the road to sponsorship success. Make no mistake about it, there are several stages on the road and each one is fraught with pitfalls. In all my researches I have never heard of a case where that first letter receives a reply like:

> Dear Mr. Bloggs,
> Thank you for your letter. What a good idea you have! Please find enclosed our cheque for £1,000,000.

It would be nice if it happened that way but alas, looking for a backer is like everything else, damned hard work.

First of all, then, we decide what the aim of the project is. It might be to sail around the world backwards or to enter the Whitbread Race. We decide what tools we need to do the job, (that is what size, shape, and material the boat should be) and the costs of building and taking part. From that we arrive at a provisional budget, a vital factor because there is no use talking to a potential sponsor unless you can quote figures and substantiate them. Notice also that I use the word "provisional". I have discovered in practice that my initial estimates for any project are below the final figures. There are so many imponderables and extras to be taken into account that if you think of every possible expense, add it all up and then add fifty per cent to the total you will be near the true figure. And even if you do think of every little item, remember we live in an inflationary society, where yesterday's penny buns cost 5p today and, who knows, tomorrow we may have little change out of a pound if we insist on indulging in such luxuries as buns. Gone are the days when my old dad in Hawick used to tell me tales of getting a packet of cigarettes and a pint of bitter for a tanner (for younger readers a tanner represents 2½p).

When we have a budget, we look at the big commercial world and try to assess who, in our opinion, will benefit from the project. At this point inside information is invaluable and is gleaned from marketing departments, advertising agencies, promotions companies, and general gossip in pubs and clubs. It may be that Blotto soap flakes are planning a big campaign around the slogan "Bring the sunshine of the Caribbean into your Monday washday". So if you are looking for a sponsor to back an expedition to search for buried treasure in the Caribbean you will have soapy and receptive ears listening to your proposition. To some extent this was the situation with the British Steel Corporation when we approached them about providing a boat for my solo voyage. They had recently launched their highly successful Steel Appeal campaign, which hinged around unusual applications for steel. They were anxious to promote steel as a versatile, attractive and durable material and saw the potential in building a round-the-world yacht.

Having chosen a company to approach, check on its financial situation. If it is making money it will be in the comfortable position of being able to listen to good ideas. If it is losing money—and many of the big ones are doing just that—it will be in no position to discuss rather obtuse ways of losing more. A quick check on the last annual report and the Chairman's Statement will therefore pay handsome dividends.

After the target is chosen, make sure that you have the right bullets and that they are properly loaded. No doubt various sponsor-seekers have various methods by which they swear. We prepare a very smart presentation in an extremely expensive leather-bound book. Terry Bond and I go to tremendous trouble with this book and, although I say it myself, when we have finished it is a masterpiece of its kind. In photographic and word form it explains the project in a straightforward way, missing out nothing but avoiding exaggeration. Perhaps most important of all, it spells out the benefits to the potential sponsor as we see them.

We work on the assumption that the man reading the presentation knows nothing about sailing, has never heard of Chay Blyth, and thinks the Round-the-World Race is an international beer-drinking marathon. But the man does know all about his company and will recognise an opportunity for publicity when he sees it.

Our efforts are therefore painstaking. First we explain the event—i.e. an international yacht race right around the world. It is unique and therefore inevitably will attract world-wide publicity. Newspapers, magazines, television networks, publishers, every conceivable media outlet will be interested and will cover it. It has drama, excitement, adventure, and there is prestige even in taking part let alone winning. I emphasise again that we never knowingly exaggerate, because statements in such a permanent document can be extracted and held against you in the future.

You must know your subject from every angle and know the answers to the questions before they are asked. That was a lesson I learned from John Dunkeley, who was Press Officer at the British Steel Corporation at the time when we announced to the world that I was going to sail single-handed westwards.

On the evening before the Press Conference, five of us sat for three hours thinking up the most diabolical questions in anticipation of the sort of thing I could be asked next day.

"Don't you think the British Steel Corporation is wasting tax-payers' money backing a man of your inexperience on such a voyage?"

"Is it not irresponsible to leave a young wife and baby, to sail deliberately into danger?"

"What do you think about Donald Crowhurst?" (That fascinating book by Nick Tomalin and Ron Hall about the Crowhurst tragedy had been published the day before).

I cannot remember the answers we worked out. The Press Conference was at the Savoy Hotel in London, and when I saw that over a hundred journalists from all over the world had gathered to hear the announcement I sweated. I need not have worried however because in the event no tough questions were asked. The point is 'though' that I was prepared if they had been.

As a self-confessed adventurer I must admit that I do not enjoy these approaches to the commercial world for money. But sponsorship is a fact of life and I therefore believe it should be tackled in a professional way. I know there is a feeling in the hallowed halls of our more traditional yacht clubs that the commercialisation of yachting is somehow to be frowned upon, even despised. I believe that such an attitude, a holier-than-thou façade that gives the impression that yachting is exclusively for the idle rich, is to be pitied.

When *British Steel* was on her early trials I sailed with four friends over to Cowes from the Hamble. It was a beautiful day, just a wisp of wind, the yacht was sailing well and the world generally looked good. Just outside Cowes we sailed gently by a yacht of similar size, her deck littered with the young and indolent rich. I can spot them a mile off. Their hair is a shade too long, slightly bleached by the sun, but immaculately parted and close to their heads. Their faces finish near to their bottom lips. They have little pot bellies and their very tatty jeans cling to their honourable bums and have cost a fortune in Kings Road.

As we went by, one of these lanky nobodies called out: "Sponsored boat, sponsored boat," and guffawed until we were out of sight. I suppose I should have been upset. Certainly one of my friends was, and gave them a time-honoured reverse Churchillian gesture. But to be honest it did not affect me because after all, almost everyone who sails a big boat is sponsored. Certainly those twitty young men had not earned the corn that had paid for their yacht. Daddy or grand-daddy had probably wheeled and dealed and possibly sweated to bring home a lot of bacon, and he was probably more than happy to spend a few thousand on a boat, if it meant that junior was out of sight.

The classic example of yacht sponsorship is Sir Francis Chichester. Lord Dulverton was his main sponsor, but there were also major commercial interests such as the International Wool Secretariat, who put up cash and kind to pay for the good knight's trips. Sir Francis was the doyen of them all because he managed to obtain sponsorship and still retain the reputation of being entirely independent and self-financed.

Even my friend, Sir Alec Rose, whose round-the-world voyage was such an inspiration to me, will be the first to admit that the commercial companies who gave him food and equipment for his trip were of invaluable help. Look too at Les Williams in *Burton Cutter* and Robin Knox Johnson in *British Oxygen*—those names were not chosen because Les likes the man who tailors his suits and Robin thinks a quick whiff of the hard stuff will help the boat sail better.

And why should it not be so? The plain fact is that no one who is without very substantial funds and a huge private income can afford to take part in big yacht racing unless he has the help of sponsorship. The ultimate was seen in the Whitbread Race when *Pen Duick VI* appeared on the start line. It was rumoured that her skipper, Eric Tabarly had a substantial grant from the French government. In addition *Pen Duick* was built in a naval yard so Eric had no worries about strikes, working-to-rule, and so on. He probably also had the naval establishment putting at his disposal such facilities as desks, secretaries, and expert advisors. The French Navy obviously have test tanks at their disposal. The list of potential help is endless.

When Tabarly lost his mast on the first leg of the race the French nation thought so much of their sailor that they immediately flew a replacement mast from France to Rio, plus experts to fix it. They were determined to have their man back in there fighting.

Contrast this situation with that facing some of the other competitors. I loaned *British Steel* to the Army free of charge but they needed a fair amount of cash to convert her from a one-berth vessel into a boat in which ten men could live and sail. To get that money they had to make a direct appeal to the public at the 1972 Earls Court Show. The Army Sailing Association also had to beg donations from a number of commercial organisations and they were helped by a large gift from an insurance company.

Roddy Ainslie, the skipper of *Second Life,* had to have money in order to compete and much of it came from the fare-paying crew members who each had to find £3,000.

Talk of such sordid matters as sponsorship grates on the ears of old school yachtsmen, but they must move with our times. If Britain wants to continue ruling the waves she has to compete against such men as Tabarly, who I would put at the top of the sailing tree. Before the Whitbread Race and even after it, I regarded Eric as the finest ocean racer the world will see this century, so he was the man I wanted to beat. He was dogged by ill-luck that time and we beat him, but I know he is a man who cannot take failure.

Now commercialism has come to yachting in a big way and personally I will lead three cheers. Even the sacred Cowes week has a sponsor and, mark my words, the day is not too far away when we will hear of the Admiral's Cup being linked with a business name.

Having waxed at some length about my theories and thoughts on sponsorship let me point out that with *Great Britain II* we did not have a commercial sponsor. When Frank Allen heard about our oil company letdown he wrote to Jack Hayward in the Bahamas telling him about it. Jack replied immediately asking Frank to contact me to let him have full details of the venture.

With the help of Terry Bond, I quickly prepared a complete dossier of the race and the sort of boat I wanted to build. Because Terry's office is in Wolverhampton and Jack Hayward is a native of that town they immediately had common ground. So a week or so after we sent the dossier out to the Bahamas, Jack telephoned Terry (actually Terry was out so he had to ring back, and his wife Carol tells me that every time the pips went he winced at the thought of the telephone bill). They talked about their mutual interest, the Wolves, who I understand are eleven young men who try to kick a piece of leather through two bits of wood, and found that they had a joint friend in Rachael Heyhoe, now Mrs. Flint, who captained the British Women's Cricket Team.

At the end of the three-minute conversation Jack said: "I think this plan of Chay's is great. I would like to be the main sponsor."

When Terry telephoned me at Newbury with the news I could hardly believe it. Was it really true? Someone whom we hardly knew and who had only met me for a brief week was going to put up the cash in such a seemingly cavalier manner? What we did not know then but were to learn as we got to know the man better was that Jack Hayward never does anything without considering it carefully. The time that had elapsed between his receiving the dossier and making the telephone call had been spent researching the project and the people concerned in it. Jack is a very rich man and has a pretty impressive organisation on call, so he was able to check on Chay Blyth and his proposition very thoroughly.

One thing he discovered was something that I had

suspected and dreaded but never been able to confirm: it was by no means certain that there would be a race at all. The two principals, Anthony Churchill and Guy Pearse, had been unable to attract a main sponsor for the race as a whole and of course, no sponsor meant no money and therefore no race. We would have looked pretty stupid spending scores of thousands on a yacht and then having no event to enter!

I am still not quite sure what happened; really it is none of my business, but suddenly there was a race organised by the Royal Naval Sailing Association and sponsored by Whitbreads. I do not know exactly what became of Anthony and Guy but suddenly they were no longer on the scene, which seemed rather a pity because they had been prime movers of the original idea. However, mine was not to reason why; we had a race and we had the money to build a boat. Things could not have looked rosier, but I know from bitter experience that such sunny weather is only the interval between the storms.

3

THE THEORY BEHIND *BRITISH STEEL* WAS SIMPLE. I WANTED A BOAT specially designed for the job, based on a proven model. I could not risk major innovations or peculiarities, I wanted a yacht well built and well designed that I knew would work before I set out on the voyage. That is why I went to Robert Clark and why *British Steel* is so similar to *Sir Thomas Lipton*. Robert had designed *Sir Thomas Lipton* and knew all her drawbacks—although they were few—and how they might be rectified. Thanks to Robert and the skills of the men at Philip's yard in Dartmouth, *British Steel* was and still is one of the greatest yachts in the world. But she was built to do a specific job and to go well to windward, and although I knew she would compete with honours, I realised she would not win in a race against the world's best.

So what kind of yacht did I need to compete in the Whitbread Race? I checked on all the yachts that had been built for ocean racing. Where possible I went to see them, where not I read avidly about them. I analysed each yacht and pictured it in my mind, and when I closed my eyes I could see it sailing. I studied race results and the speeds that had been achieved, and always one name kept cropping up—*Windward Passage*.

Here was a very special yacht. It was born in the mind of the late Robert F. Johnson, an American, and in 1968 he and his son, Robert Mark Johnson, created their own boatyard in Freeport, Grand Bahamas, to build the boat. They did a magnificent job and she was finished in early 1969 just in time for the Southern Ocean Racing Conference. She entered and won every race she competed in.

After that *Windward Passage* went on to set a new record in the Miami—Jamaica Race. The next major event was the 1969 Honolulu Race where she finished first and set a new elapsed time record, which unfortunately was taken away from Mr. Johnson Senior by the Transpac Committee, who penalised him two hours for a starting line infringement. The penalty caused a furore in yachting circles at the time but like all big-deal happenings it soon blew over. Certainly the loss of the record did nothing to slow the progress of *Windward Passage*. When Robert Johnson died in the autumn of 1969, his son took over as owner and skipper and continued to race with distinction. When last I checked *Windward Passage* held the following records:

Miami—Nassau Race
Miami—Jamaica Race
California Coastal Race
Transpacific Yacht Race

She also finished first in all the Southern Ocean Racing Conference races and won the Bermuda Race, the Acapulco Race, the La Paz Race and the Honolulu Race. The last achievement was perhaps the greatest of all because she was the first boat in history to win Class "A" and the race overall.

The designer of *Windward Passage* is Alan Gurney, an Englishman who has a New York office and commutes regularly. He had designed a yacht 70 feet overall in length and in principle like a large dinghy in that she is very flat. She is a light displacement vessel built of wood and although

I wanted glass fibre, I knew that the theories would not vary too much.

So I set about contacting Mr. Gurney and asking him to design me a yacht on similar lines to *Windward Passage* but faster. I remember our first conversation quite distinctly. I was in Plymouth giving a lecture at the Royal Western Yacht Club for International Paints, who had done such a fantastic paint job on *British Steel.* They had given their men and know-how to paint her and the pristine state in which she returned to home waters was a tribute to their skills.

Anyway, the conversation was not very long because, as I was soon to discover, A. Gurney Esq., is a man of few words. I recall my transatlantic telephone call verbatim:

> Me: Hello, can I speak to Alan Gurney please?
>
> A.G.: Speaking.
>
> Me: My name is Chay Blyth. We have never met but I have heard of you.
>
> A.G.: I have heard of you too.
>
> Me: That's very kind. There's a round-the-world race for yachts being organised and I wonder if you would be interested in designing a yacht for me so that I can compete?
>
> A.G.: Yes.
>
> Me: I want a boat similar to *Windward Passage* but I want to be faster than her and I want all the snags in her ironed out in it. Do you think you could do that for me?
>
> A.G.: Yes.
>
> Me: Good. I will fly out within the next two or three days and we can discuss it.
>
> A.G.: Fine. Goodbye.

Obviously not in line for the title of the World's Filibuster Champion, Alan is undoubtedly one of the finest designers of ocean yachts and I counted myself lucky to get his services. As things turned out I could not fly to the States, so I wrote to him explaining in more detail the sort of yacht I wanted. He replied that he would undertake the commission and was coming over to Britain. We met at the Royal Ocean Racing Club in London and there was an immediate affinity. He is a small, quiet and pleasant man, looking more like a refugee professor than an ocean racing expert.

Alan had brought a drawing of *Windward Passage* with him and we pored for hours over it, discussing her advantages and shortcomings. I explained my hopes for the race, my desire for line honours, the Elapsed Time Prize and if possible the Handicap Prize.

"I am excited by the project, Chay," said Alan. "But before I start work I want you to understand one thing."

"What's that?" I asked in all innocence.

"I'm very expensive," he replied.

I asked him how much he would charge to design the boat and to produce all the working drawings and he was right—he is very expensive. It is a good job I have always maintained that one has to pay for the best.

Having commissioned Alan Gurney and with a main sponsor in Jack Hayward, my next task was to find a builder. Alan and I had agreed on foam sandwich construction (a filling of expanded polystyrene between two layers of glass fibre) because this would give us light displacement and therefore speed. I talked with a former boat builder, Derek Kelsall, about the method of construction because I was assured that he was an expert in the field, and eventually I invited him to work on the project in a consultancy capacity. With him on board it was possible for most yacht building yards in Britain to undertake the job.

I must admit that I had automatically assumed that Philip and Son would build the yacht. They had done a remarkable job in building *British Steel* and I had grown to rely upon them and to respect their work. I wrote and asked if they could undertake the building of the new yacht and they said that they could, so Alan Gurney, Derek Kelsall and I travelled down to Dartmouth armed with details and drawings.

As I always say, every silver lining hides a damned great black cloud and we came face to face with it when the man in charge at the yard said: "Sorry, Chay. We can't do it. Your yacht is three feet too big. We have developed a production line for our regular work and to fit in your boat we would have to move the entire production line. It just can't be done, old son."

Here was the first major problem and we thought of every way round it. Derek pointed to a spot in the corner of the yard and asked if it was available. It was, but the Philip's men were not too happy about us using it because they knew from their *British Steel* experience that the world's Press would be swarming round to take photographs at every stage of construction and as this part of the yard was particularly grotty they felt it would be bad for their image.

In the end we decided upon the erection of a temporary building using heavy-gauge polythene. It would not have been ideal but it would have sufficed.

Then came the real nitty-gritty. The price. I had a budget which I had shown to Jack Hayward and although it was something of a "guesstimate" it was based soundly upon experience and reliable information. For the construction of the hull and deck I had allocated £30,000 to £34,000. I had actually had a quote from another company for £25,000 but because the outfit was very small and did not really have the right facilities I was not keen to go to them.

Obviously I could not expect a firm price from Philip's there and then so, having ironed out the wheres and hows of the situation, I left the yard feeling reasonably happy. As Captain Mainwaring in "Dad's Army" keeps saying to Private Pike—Stupid Boy! When I telephoned the then managing director of Philip and Son, Tony Smith, a couple of days later he said: "I've got a bit of a shock for you, Chay. The hull and deck will cost you £68,000."

"No, no Tony," I said patiently. "You mean £68,000 for the whole boat."

"No Chay. For the hull and deck only."

Goodness knows how they arrived at that figure. No

doubt they had their reasons and it is true that they would have to buy in special materials to do the job. But £68,000! I began to think a solid gold yacht would have been cheaper. At that price it was just not on, and I was certainly not going to ask Jack Hayward or any of the other people involved to help with such an exorbitant project.

So we were without a builder. My initial reaction was: "Oh Lord, we have been through all this before." When we got the go-ahead for *British Steel* we had to get a 59 foot yacht built in three months and poor Maureen had spent literally eight hours a day five days a week phoning around Britain to find a builder. The Dartmouth yard had been our saviours then but this time they most certainly were not.

I started to ring round myself and it was even worse than before. Every yacht building yard I contacted was chock-a-block with work. They were snowed under and the reason was that Value Added Tax was soon to be introduced and at that time boats and caravans were exempt from purchase tax. By getting work done pre-V.A.T. you could save a fortune so every builder had full order books. Here was poor old Chay with a race, a sponsor, a design, and no boat.

It was not a time for the faint hearted. We had a discussion and decided to consider building the boat ourselves. We would form a company and employ our own labour, find a suitable building and get cracking. It was the ultimate in do-it-yourself, a desperate remedy for a desperate situation. But it was an idea fraught with difficulties. For example, should the company make a profit? Think about it. If it was a normal, commercial company owned in part by me, was it fair to the sponsor and to all the many companies who gave materials and equipment, for me to make a profit out of them? On the other hand how do you operate a company to break exactly even? And would it be reasonable to the other individuals involved in the company to tell them that there would be no profits at the end? And would we get the right sort of labour if we only intended to employ men for a limited period? Finally we decided to forget it.

Fortunately the demise of the do-it-yourself idea coincided with a decision by Derek Kelsall to go back into business on his own account and he wrote saying that he would undertake the construction of the hull and deck at the budget price. He searched around for suitable premises and was lucky to find a building adjoining the estuary at Sandwich in Kent. It was close to his home and therefore ideal for him.

While the lofting—preparation for the actual construction—was taking place Terry Bond and I began to contact firms for equipment and materials. Where possible we wanted the goods free or at a substantial discount but we did not beg or plead. We explained the nature of the venture, the sort of publicity it would attract, and asked politely for their help and co-operation.

I am delighted to say that many suppliers were fired with enthusiasm for the project. It would be impossible to list them all but some I recall with particular gratitude.

Internationally-known companies such as Ford who gave us a superb engine and Marconi who loaned us the latest radio telephone equipment, proved that no matter how large the organisation, there is still the will to join in an adventurous project. It is not just the goods that they provide, but the know-how as well. Their advice and the care with which they install their products is invaluable. The same goes for suppliers like International Paints, who are blessed with executives like Eddie Whiting, who is such a genuine and pleasant fellow that whenever we neglected to wash the boat down I felt we were personally insulting him.

But as well as the household names we had help from the specialist firms. A Rochdale company called Turner Bros., (Asbestos) Limited gave us all we wanted as far as rovings were concerned. Mr. N. S. Broome, managing director of Scott Bader Company Limited of Wellingborough, agreed to supply our need for polyester resin. Thames Plywood Manufacturers gave us all our marine ply at fifty per cent of the normal price.

The lists are endless and I do not want to sound like a public relations officer, but the fact is that firms like these deserve the praise for any success we may have achieved because their encouragement and advice as well as their top quality products enabled us to have confidence in our craft.

★ ★ ★

While the yacht building preliminaries were going on I was facing other related problems, not the least of which was a crew.

Any major yacht race, particularly a new venture like this, is initially going to attract plenty of entries. The organisers have enquiries falling around them like confetti as people with actual or dreamed-of yachts forget such mundane matters as taking time off work, finding crews, finance, families, and so on. There is however a subtle change as the start of the race draws near. All the arguments against going take on an unpleasant reality. For example, who can afford to take twelve months off work? It has to be a year because of the training involved, and remember you are not able to telephone the office every day or issue instant orders if a crisis arises back at home. And even if you have the money to buy or build a suitable yacht the expense does not end there. Do not forget food for yourself and the crew for 52 weeks. And spares. And the cost of repairs and labour in such expensive ports as Rio. And the cost of keeping families and homes back in Britain.

Perhaps the biggest problem however is the crew. The skipper must rely on finding people who, like himself, can take a year away from their commitments and this narrows the field considerably. Another requirement is that they are physically and mentally fit, so again you are reducing your potential crew members. Finally they must be dedicated enough to become and remain an integral part of the team. All these factors mean that it is extremely unlikely that any skipper will find his ideal crew, and may well have to settle for second best.

However, there is one group of people who can count among their numbers men who satisfy every requirement, the men of Her Majesty's Forces. Nowadays the Services are keen on adventure training and, I thought to myself, here was a classic opportunity made to measure for them. The Services had asked me for the loan of *British Steel*. Dare I ask them for the loan of a crew?

I laid my plans carefully. The loan of *British Steel* to the Army was nearing finalisation and I went to a meeting with Brigadier Oliver Roome and Major Neil Calier to dot the i's and cross the t's. Basically the agreement was simple. The Army could borrow the yacht without charge for the duration of the race and for the period leading up to it. It would be their responsibility to carry out the necessary conversions and to get her shipshape. Neil, who was organising the whole project for the Army, was over the moon because as far as he was concerned it was a perfect arrangement. The only proviso I made was that a friend of mine, Brian Cooke, who is manager of the National Westminster in Parkstone, Poole, could use *British Steel* first in the solo Transatlantic Race. Brian had been hoping to have a boat of his own but his sponsorship had fallen through and because I had it in my power to lend him the boat I was happy to do so. He is a fine sailor and I knew he would look after her.

With all the wrinkles ironed out the Brigadier, Neil, and I shook hands and talked of other things. I was careful not to mention my thoughts on taking a Service crew at that stage because I knew that the man who could best say yea or nay was General Sir Michael Carver, Admiral of the Army Sailing Association and the man who had telegraphed me initially asking to borrow *British Steel*. The very last meeting in the charter saga was with the General, the Brigadier, the Major, and me, and it took the form of a lunch at the Belgium Club. It was a good lunch, made all the better by my secret thoughts on the situation in which I found myself. There was I, Sgt. Chay Blyth (Ret.), as a guest of the Chief of the General Staff. Oh boy! If they could see me now, those paratrooper friends of mine! I thought it was quite hilarious and the more I thought about it the harder it was to keep my face straight. Sgt. Blyth, choking down the port and giving his erudite opinion on matters of the moment. The three officers were nodding sagely, adding their much more considered opinions, and remaining inscrutable. I wish I knew what they had really been thinking—or perhaps I don't.

I was careful not to drink too much wine because my mind had to be crystal clear when I popped the question. My crew just had to be soldiers, not only because they could be allocated the time but for a hundred additional reasons. They were mentally and physically trained to withstand the situation I knew we would encounter. They would be basically equipped with their normal Army gear. There would probably be a store available so that we would have somewhere to leave equipment. Transport would be easier. Everyone would be together in one place. The advantages were endless.

Ideally I wanted paratroopers because I know them and the way they think. Paras have a common denominator and are fiercely proud of their Brigade. Wherever the Brigade had been in the world, whatever famous or infamous incidents have befallen paras collectively or individually, every soldier in the Brigade would know about it. You have only to say: "Remember Borneo?" and every para has a related mental image. The same applies to Cyprus or Aden or Aldershot, and the mention of a place or a person triggers off a string of anecdotes.

What a tremendous advantage this is over a "mixed" crew, condemned to spend months together in the confines of a yacht. Imagine an accountant sitting on deck sewing a sail and saying: "Goodness me, I had a terrible time trying to work out the Corporation Tax for such-and-such a company." He is talking to another crew member, a bloke who might be a radio technician, and he is half listening just waiting to get in with his conversation stopper about the whoop whoop valves that fluttered and died. With those men the only common chord is sailing, whereas the paras share so much.

As we ate that lunch in the Belgium Club I twisted the conversation this way and that trying to create exactly the right environment in which to make my approach to the General. Schweppes' training had taught me that there is always "just the right moment". I had formulated the exact sentences in my mind and although I say it myself it is at moments like these that I am fairly cool. I have an aim and I evolve a plan to achieve it. At last, as we approached the dregs of the coffee, I was ready. I told General Carver that I too wanted to enter the race and that I thought I had a sponsor for a new boat. Then I said: "Would the Army look favourably on me taking an Army crew? And would you pass the coffee please, I would love another cup." The plan was to slip in the request and follow it immediately with a distraction.

The General, bless his heart, said: "Oh, I'm sure that we would look favourably on the request Chay," passed the coffee and went on to talk about something else. I relaxed and honestly cannot remember anything more about the luncheon. I was sure that an officer and a gentleman never went back on his word.

What I had not told the General was that I wanted a crew of paras from the same unit, and unlike the other Services crews, I did not want to change them at each port of call. One crew going all the way round would provide much needed continuity, and we would be able to cut down on administration.

I dashed straight home after the lunch and Maureen got out the typewriter. I wrote to Brigadier Tony Ward Booth, then Commander of the 16th Independent Parachute Brigade Group.

> Dear Brigadier Ward Booth,
>
> I am entering a yacht in the forthcoming Round-the-World Race and I am hoping to have it crewed by Service personnel. I had lunch today with General Carver and he indicated that it may be possible to have the necessary men. Ideally I would like the entire crew to be paratroopers. . .

The Brigadier replied by return, saying he was absolutely delighted and assuring me of the Brigade's complete co-operation.

I had my crew.

* * *

I learned sailing by getting into a boat and disappearing over the horizon. I felt sure that given two sustained months at sea any paratrooper who was physically fit, determined, and keen, would become a competent ocean racing crewman. The first month would be utilised in explaining the theories and getting acclimatised to the boat. The second month would be spent on the seas, racing.

The crew for the new yacht—it had not got a name at this stage—should ideally be between twelve and eighteen strong. I explained this to the Brigadier, but added that initially I wanted twenty men so that I could have a crew plus reserves. The liaison officer for the project as far as the paras were concerned was Captain David Gay, a Royal Artillery Para officer, and he quickly emerged as a lynchpin of the operation. The amount of work and enthusiasm that he generated was quite incredible.

Together we drafted a notice board memo to be circulated around the Brigade. It explained briefly the details of the race and also that I was not necessarily looking for men who had sailing experience. The only qualification was that they had to have been parachute soldiers for a minimum of two years. Rank did not matter, neither did age. From all units of the Parachute Brigade volunteer applications started to pour in. They came from a battalion in Cyprus and another in Northern Ireland, from Scotland and England and all over the place—altogether we had over 300 volunteers.

How to sort them out? No doubt there were more subtle and efficient ways than mine, but I doubt whether there were quicker ways, because my method was to arrange a series of meetings sprung quickly and unexpectedly on the applicants. Those who did not turn up and had not got a very good excuse indeed were struck off the list. It was a rough and ready system but it was impossible for me to interview 300 men, it would have taken at least half-an-hour per man and I had not got the time.

So what did I consider a reasonable excuse for not turning up? Well, a broken neck might just about qualify, but the fact that it was your wife's birthday and you had promised to take her out to dinner was certainly not accepted. This trip had to become a religion with the crew.

The initial thinning out cut the numbers down to a manageable fifty and in-depth interviews gave me twenty.

The first stage in the training I had carefully worked out was to go to Scotland for a Compatibility Course christened "Exercise Dry Sail". I have a large two bedroomed cottage about ten miles from my home town of Hawick. It stands in the middle of a fenced-off Forestry Commission forest and is about three miles from the nearest other house. Apart from the bedrooms there are two living rooms, a kitchen, and a bathroom. There is pumped water and electricity and very little else. It was here at my beloved cottage that the twenty of us spent a fortnight. Communication with the outside world was forbidden. No papers, no television, no radio. Even post was banned and I well remember one day the startled postman, fed up with having to trail all the way to the cottage with what turned out to be the final demand for the electricity bill to be paid, scratching his head in classic style as he encountered two men who instead of passing the time of day with him turned and ran away. They knew the penalty for having conversation with an outsider.

Basically the idea was to test how individuals would get on with each other, and how they would adapt to the restrictions of a confined space. Each man had a small space in one room allocated to him, a camp bed, and a set amount of kit. I was trying to simulate the conditions they would experience on a boat. (Ideally the exercise should have been carried out on a boat but I had not got one available so the cottage was the next best thing). In fact the conditions were as near perfect as possible because there was one lavatory, one bath, a shortage of water, and twenty blokes living in three rooms. Every man had to make down his camp bed each morning and make it up again at night. All clothes were to be kept in the individual's three-foot-square space and the whole cottage had to be maintained in a spotlessly clean condition. A dirty mark, a sock out of place, and the man responsible was for the high jump.

A typical day started at 7.30 a.m. when we would all get up and go for a five mile run. At 8.30 a.m. we would "splash down" which meant a quick swill rather than a good wash because all the water had to be pumped. We would also have a shave. (Baths were one per person per week).

Breakfast was at nine and initially we took it in turns to cook. I split the men into two teams, one called the Starboard Watch and the other the Port Watch. I appointed a Watch Officer of the Day and he had to organise the cooking. Generally the food was quite well prepared considering we were amateurs, but towards the end of the fortnight I experimented by appointing a full time Cook Orderly who was responsible for all meals. It transpired that having one man to do the job was best for continuity.

At ten o'clock we had lessons. Two weeks before we set off for my cottage I had given each man a subject and told him to learn as much as he could about it and to be prepared to give a lesson on the subject to the rest of the potential crew. Usually the men started off by knowing nothing whatsoever about their subject, which varied from rigging and splicing to tides and public relations. To my delight everyone took the job seriously and we all learned a great deal from this part of the exercise. The chaps had done their homework well and the question-and-answer sessions afterwards were extremely valuable. A good example of the trouble that the lecturers went to was the oldest man in the group, Captain Brian Daniels, who had to prepare a lesson on the use of the sextant. He had to explain how to take angles and to find a ship's position by using the instrument, so before the move up to Scotland he went into Aldershot and paid something around £17 for a plastic model of a sextant simply to use as an aid for his lecture.

These classroom sessions lasted for two hours and then we had Pottering Time. The men could wander off and do what they liked, go for a walk, sit and look at the burn, or even build a new fence around the cottage! There were other little maintenance jobs too and I will be forever grateful to those kind paratroopers who felt moved to use their Pottering Time to carry out repairs and improvements to the cottage. It may not be generally known that I am not the keenest of do-it-yourselfers, in fact at home if there is a nail to be knocked in or a car to be washed I believe in calling in the experts. There was honestly no coercion but as that fence sprung up around the cottage and as the wallop went on the walls it did my old heart good.

After a light lunch there was another two-hour lesson on a different subject and this was followed by strenuous physical exercise such as tug-of-war or a game of soccer.

The evening meal was prepared, eaten with varying degrees of relish depending on who had been the cook, the dishes were washed up, and by eight o'clock it was pitch black outside and the twenty of us were sitting there with absolutely nothing to do. To me this was perhaps the most interesting time, because a prime objective of "Exercise Dry Sail" was to discover how the men reacted to boredom and the pressures of living on top of one another. Privacy for more than a few minutes each day was impossible and no matter how crochety or insular you felt, there was no way of getting away from the others.

These nowhere-to-go-and-nothing-to-do periods were occupied in different ways by different characters. Cards and chess were excellent time killers and quite a few opted for them. Small talk soon became boring and within a couple of days no one could think of any more jokes. I believe that humour is an essential ingredient of any relationship and we really did have some laughs. One night little Len Price, who was destined eventually to become helmsman on the boat, stood up around nine o'clock and without a word shaved, washed, combed his tousled hair and put on his best bib and tucker.

"Where the hell do you think you are going?" I asked, watching him in amazement.

"I'm going to have a night out, skipper," he replied. "I thought I would visit Pete Bates in the next bedroom."

That was funny enough but the joke continued and spread. Len was made most welcome by Pete and his room-mates, who were all of four yards across the landing. Their hospitality was warm if frugal (the cottage was almost "dry ship" with only one nip and a single beer per night allowed) and they yarned until late into the night. The visit ended with a reciprocal invitation for the following night and always there was the pantomine of sprucing up and dressing in best clobber before going round to the neighbours.

Another way I had of breaking the evening monotony was to have an organised discussion. I always put one man in charge and he was carefully briefed to make sure that everyone became involved.

The main discussion subject was usually chosen by me and I would write down a number of questions and areas which I wanted explored. Where possible the subject would be as controversial as possible. For example, we discussed the situation in Northern Ireland and in particular the incident that has become known as "Bloody Sunday". The main question I posed was, in view of the circumstances as we knew them—and because of the paratrooper grapevine we knew far more than the ordinary man-in-the-street—was the killing of thirteen people excessive? The arguments were callous and compassionate but always fascinating. As the evening wore on the debate often became heated and the atmosphere electric. It was the debate chairman's job to keep things under control and this he usually managed to do, at least I cannot recall any serious physical injuries that resulted from a discussion.

A difference between these and the conventional debate

was that usually we did not have a vote at the end. Voting on matters which one cannot directly influence seems rather pointless to me, particularly when one is making a decision without knowing all the facts. I am all in favour of men having firm opinions and expressing them, but what is the point of discovering that fifteen out of twenty-five men are in favour of capital punishment? After a two-hour discussion they cannot possibly have discovered all the facts, they have not had access to statistics, and they are not qualified to make a definite decision. I am all for democracy but I think a referendum on any subject can possibly result in a wrong decision being made.

However, things were very different when we discussed taking Sue, a super girl from the World Expeditionary Association, along on the trip as cook. Here was a subject white-hot with controversy and the fors and againsts mounted up like legions ready to go into battle.

The initial reaction is: Christ! Think of the problems. All those men living together for months and only one girl on board. Because we are all sex orientated everyone immediately thinks of sex. I am no Freud and I am not sure of the exact reasons, but I do think we are unconsciously influenced by television, advertising, newspapers, and conversation aimed at transmitting sex images. However, the world of the media is a world of make-believe and thank God the real thing is just not like that. Sane and moral people simply do not think about sex for the whole of their waking life. Please do not think I am against it, I am as much a fan of sex as the next man, but there is a time and a place for everything and I do know that there is a world of difference between a warm and cosy bed and the rocking, pitching, damp environment of a boat.

Nevertheless, first thoughts are of sex and I admit that my initial reaction was that if we took Sue along one of the lads would soon be trying to chat her up, she may fall for one of them and there would be jealousies and pettiness. More mature thought on my part told me though that this situation would not arise because we would not be taking just any old girl. Sue Manderson is a young woman full of character, she already had a fiancé, and I was sure in my own mind that she could have coped with the situation. My wife Maureen, too, would have fitted well into the scheme of things, but I had already discussed the possibilities with her and we had decided that because of Samantha she would stay at home this time.

So the discussion at the cottage started. The Starboard Watch sat on one side of the table, The Port Watch on the other. I sat at the head of the table and announced the subject: "Gentlemen, we will now debate whether to take a girl cook, Sue Manderson, with us." While they collected their thoughts and opinions, I painted in some of Sue's background. She was twenty-four, well educated, much travelled, engaged to be married, a pleasant personality with a thirst for adventure. Although I was not convinced that she should come, I described her ambition in glowing terms because I wanted to counteract the anti-feeling that the initial sex picture was bound to conjure up with the men.

The points were made forcibly. Would the wives and girl friends of the crew get aggro and would that be an understandable reaction? Would the other members of the crew feel inhibited by having a girl on board? What sort of privacy would she expect? Would she really prove a temptation? Were we breaking our vow to be an all-para crew? Would we still qualify as a Services entry? What would it do to our image?

I had private reasons for wanting a girl to be considered. There is no doubt that a female on board provides a stablising factor. Men are better behaved, better dressed, and there is less swearing. They are also more careful about their habits and their attitudes.

The discussion went on until the small hours of the morning and my last question was grossly unfair: "Being paratroopers, were we self-disciplined, highly trained, and dedicated enough to make sure that no girl or other influence could affect our objective—to win the race?" The answer had to be yes and it brought a successful end to the discussion. This time, though, I decided to climax the debate with a vote because the men had heard all the arguments and were entitled to make a decision. Eight men voted for inviting Sue to join us, twelve were against it. I have already said that I believe in democracy so Sue did not become part of the team. When I told her she was extremely disappointed.

By the middle of the second week in Scotland things were really beginning to happen, and true characters and personalities were emerging. Defences were down, nerves were twanging, and I began deliberately and ruthlessly to explore minds and attitudes. I had one man there—even now it would be more than my life is worth to reveal to the others who it was—in whom I had complete trust. The majority of the paratroopers had only known me for a few weeks and were understandably rather wary of me. I had made it clear that there was only one captain and because they were used to discipline and taking orders they regarded me as authority and would shy away from a confrontation with me. I therefore used my aide to provoke situations. If I wanted to test a man I thought was weak, I would give my "secret agent" the nod to deliberately pick an argument with him by disagreeing with whatever he was saying. The weak man would invariably get ratty at the slightest provocation and this meant that he was not suitable for the trip, because we had been taught in one of the morning lessons that to avoid an argument one should move away from it on to another subject, and the weak man had not been listening to the teacher.

Such an attitude on my part may seem hard and even underhand. I defend it because I had to choose the right men. I was undoubtedly going to change their lives and I had to be sure that they could cope with the change and be better men for it. I had to bear in mind that they were soldiers just as I had been a few years previously. They had unconsciously enjoyed the anonymity of the British Army but now I was going to be responsible for placing them firmly in the public eye. They were going to be in charge of one of the fastest ocean racing yachts the world has ever known, sailing in the most ambitious race ever organised. The Press and television would want to interview them, because when they set foot ashore they would be news.

Another formidable situation they would have to face would be when they were guests at some of the world's most exclusive yacht clubs. The majority of clubs are welcoming but we must face the fact that some are rather snooty and their members can give the impression of being aloof. The occasional big boat owner with pots of money considers himself somehow superior. Although the attitude mystifies and amuses me, I have learned to live with it, but for my crew it would be a new experience.

The snooty sailors are adept at taking the mickey and I wanted a crew who, in a quiet and dignified way, could view these snobs in their correct perspective and not be hurt or humbled by them.

Do not mistake my motives, I was much more worried for the snobs than for my crew. The paratrooper is a highly trained man geared towards aggression. In my worst imaginings I saw one of the chaps, stung by a snob, saying, "Right mate. You, me, outside!" One bang and it would have been over.

I was going to have to introduce my crew to situations divorced from actual sailing and they had to be able to cope. Another personal worry was that after the race, when they had been exposed to the limelight and hospitality, would they be satisfied with their lot? They would have to go back to being soldiers, privates, sergeants, and so on, but would they become dissatisfied and yearn for the good life again? There would be parties before we set sail, lavish banquets in Cape Town, Sydney, and Rio, and through it all I was determined that my crew would be ambassadors for Britain and the Parachute Brigade. Therefore when I assessed each man and his ability to cope with a social situation it was as much a measure of his fitness to be a crew member as his physical and sailing accomplishments.

Incidentally, I am often asked whether when making my crew choice I ever considered an individual's marital status and if, following the American business executive appointment system, I interviewed his wife or girl friend. The answer is that I did not consider it. It was of no interest to me whether a man was single, engaged, married, or living tally. Servicemen will understand why, but for those who have not done their bit for Her Majesty let me explain. Eight months, the period of the voyage, might seem a long time to the civvy to be parted from his loved one, but remember, many of these men had served in Bahrein or some similarly outlandish place for up to twelve months. I did two tours myself. Some of the men with me in Scotland served in such danger zones as Northern Ireland and their nearest and dearest knew the situation and accepted it. On reflection the men were probably a damned sight safer with me than with their unit.

We were scheduled to stay in Scotland for a full three weeks but by the end of the second week I had everything I needed to know about each man. I decided that of the twenty who had attended the Compatibility Course I would drop four. One night I told everyone to be ready to leave early the next morning and then I told the unlucky four. Three of them took the news as paratroopers should, disappointed but realising that I had my reasons and accepting the fact. The fourth laddie was not so stoical. When I told him he slammed out of the room, crashed the door behind him, and shouted: "You can stick your ——— cruise up your ——." Never mind, I thought, Captain Bligh had the same trouble and thank goodness I had sorted the wheat from the chaff before we set sail.

If I was happy that I had secured my crew, I was far from joyful about the boat building situation when we returned from Scotland. The schedule at Derek Kelsall's Sandwich yard had fallen way behind. He told me that labour was virtually impossible to hire, small items were not available, and I also discovered that for various reasons some firms would not supply the builders' materials unless they were paid in advance.

An emergency meeting of the crew was convened. I

explained the position and pulled no punches because I needed their help not only to sail the boat but to build it as well. To a man they co-operated. They took all the leave and the weekends that were due to them and worked in shifts literally round the clock as labourers. Every moment that God sent, Saturdays and Sundays, high days and holidays, up to 20 hours a day they grafted on jobs that they had never touched before. The conditions, with the stinging slivers of glass fibre eating and irritating through clothes and skin, were desperate and yet they never complained and never slacked. Quite frankly without this voluntary work by the crew the yacht would never have reached the start line. I began to realise just how lucky I was and to thank the stars that my rather rough and ready selection system had somehow thrown up a bunch of eighteen carat gold nuggets.

4

One of the perks of being a sponsor in the yachting world is that you can choose the name of the boat you are buying. Some race organisers draw the line at blatant advertising, but I fear they are fighting a rearguard action because it is an obvious and direct way for the sponsor to achieve publicity and therefore justify his expenditure. Among recent examples are *British Steel, Kriter, Burton Cutter, Strongbow, British Oxygen*, and the not-so-obvious *FT*—backed with *Financial Times* money.

With Jack Hayward, however, we had a very different situation because he is a modest man who is not over-keen on personal publicity. The last thing he would have wanted would have been a yacht name that directly associated the project with him, in fact, if I had even suggested that the yacht should be called the *Jack Hayward*, he would have withdrawn his sponsorship.

The matter began to resolve itself during a dinner I had in London with two long-standing friends, John Dunkeley who was then Press Officer of the British Steel Corporation, and one of his assistants Phil Wolfinden. The real reason for the meeting was to test their reaction to the Army's suggestion that the name of *British Steel* should be changed to *British Soldier* and typically the steel men were magnanimous about it. They said that it was now my yacht, and while they were pleased that I had consulted them, they felt I could do what I liked with the boat and anyway they had no objection to the name change. I hesitate from heaping praise on folk because it may sound like gratitude, but I can say hand over heart that John and Phil and indeed everyone I have ever met at the British Steel Corporation are A1 people.

I am delighted to say that they have A1 brains too. As we were talking about yacht names the conversation naturally arrived at the possibilities for a name for my new vessel.

"Who is launching it?" asked John Dunkeley.

"No idea," I replied. "Jack and I haven't discussed the matter."

In fact it was one of the many matters that Jack and I had not discussed because with him resident in the Bahamas and me spending most of my time in an out-of-the-way boatyard direct communication was almost impossible. Add to this the fact that Jack has an apparent aversion to writing letters and you can see the problems we faced.

We bandied names around for a while and then Phil, a wise head on young shoulders, said: "Why don't you ask Princess Anne?"

I cannot recall ever before being tempted to shout Eureka! but this time it was the only reaction I could find to Phil's inspiration.

"Better still, why not call the yacht the *Princess Anne*?" said John.

It was indeed a near-brilliant idea and the only doubt we had was that the name Princess Anne would probably be reserved for a huge aircraft carrier or a luxury cruiser. Nevertheless, it was certainly worth a try and when I got home I couldn't wait to phone Jack Hayward. He thought the idea of asking Princess Anne to perform the launching ceremony was fabulous.

But would the Princess be so enthusiastic? My hopes were pinned on the fact that she just might remember our first meeting. With the Duke of Edinburgh and Prince Charles she had been at the Hamble to greet me when I had returned from my solo voyage and it was the most memorable day of my life. I realised that for the Princess, her constant list of engagements must merge into one with time, but she would probably remember the occasion if only because of the cheeky young Scotsman all the hoo-ha was about. . .

During the buffet that followed the return I stood opposite Princess Anne and I could not stop myself from staring at her. It was becoming embarrassing but I could not help it so eventually by way of explanation I leaned over and said: "Ma'am, I hope you will not mind me saying this, and I promise it is meant as a compliment, but you are much more beautiful than your photographs." I am unashamedly a passionate Royalist and for my money Princess Anne is the fairest of them all. She is one of the most attractive women I have ever met and Captain Mark Phillips is a very lucky man.

Fortunately the Princess took my gauche remark in the spirit in which it was meant, smiled broadly, and promptly told her father. It was a good thing that he too has a sense of humour because thinking about it afterwards I could see that the whole thing could easily have been misconstrued.

There is an etiquette in all things formal, particularly when one makes an approach to Buckingham Palace. I believe in professionalism at all times, so I insisted that my request to Princess Anne, that she might consider launching the new yacht, should be done in the correct way. In this I was guided as always by my friend Patrick McNair Wilson, who is Member of Parliament for the New Forest which even now is considered a safe Tory seat. Patrick is ex-Eton and the Guards, I am ex-Hawick High School and the Paras, nevertheless he is my sort of man. I looked up the word "urbane" and according to my pocket dictionary it means "refined; suave; courteous". Patrick is all of these things and he combines them with a sense of humour and a sense of public relations that is second to none.

He told us the correct procedure for our approach to the Palace and the information we should submit with the request, drawings of the boat, suggested dates, venue, and so on.

I wrote to the Palace and had my first taste of the sheer speed and efficiency of the place. It must be one of the best run organisations in the world and should be a model on which British industry could build a brighter future. The reply from Miss Rowena Brassey, Lady in Waiting to Princess Anne, was immediate and I am delighted to say it was in the affirmative. Her Royal Highness would be happy to launch the boat on May 21st, 1973. I was over the moon. I telephoned Jack Hayward immediately and he shared my excitement.

But as the launch date drew nearer so I became more and more concerned. It was obvious that the boat would be nowhere near ready. Even the valiant efforts of the crew could not bring the building back on programme and as May dawned I was all for contacting the Princess and asking her to postpone the date. Frank Allen, who was making all the arrangements for the launch, and Terry Bond, who was liaising with Buckingham Palace, counselled against a postponement and in retrospect they were right. It would have been most inconvenient, the Princess would probably not have been free on another date, there would have been inevitable bad publicity, and the boat building would lose its sense of urgency. I believe in listening to reasoned arguments and if they sound correct there is no disgrace in changing one's mind. May 21st it was.

The arrangements to be made for a Royal occasion are unbelievable. Certainly one man could not tackle the event and fortunately again friends came to my aid. Frank Allen was fantastic, bringing his acute sense of business to the affair, convening meetings of Ramsgate Corporation, drawing up guest lists, sending out invitations, liaising with official bodies and police and bands and caterers and goodness knows who.

Terry reckons that he helped too but it occurs to me that he had all the perks such as travelling in the Queen's Flight helicopter to inspect the landing site and making numerous visits to Buckingham Palace to discuss arrangements with the authorities there. (It is a rumour without foundation that he organised coach loads of his relatives and public relations clients to stand in the Mall and watch him drive nonchalantly through the big black iron gates of the Palace).

Invaluable help came too from Lord Astor, President of *The Times* Newspapers. As Lord Lieutenant of Kent he was to act as host to the Princess on her visit to the county and his experience in matters of protocol was faultless.

Despite all this help there were many items left until the last minute and one of these was the choosing of a name for the yacht. As we had anticipated the *Princess Anne* was not really acceptable to the Palace so Jack Hayward and I sat down and drew up endless lists of possible names, considered them all and then rejected them. We agreed that the name had to be non-commercial and that if possible it should reflect the reason why we were all involved in the project. It is at times like these, when you are just about to rip out hair and settle for "The Thing" as a name, that inspiration is needed. Rarely do I have the magic but I am lucky enough to meet people who do and this time the man with divine guidance was Jack Hayward.

"How about *Great Britain II*?" he asked. It was so obviously right there was no need for discussion.

A minor problem is that a boat cannot be named after another boat unless the owner of the new boat owns the original. What this means is that you have to own the *Queen Mary* before you can register *Queen Mary II* or *Queen Mary III*. We surmounted this obstacle because Jack had been responsible for financing the return of S.S. *Great Britain* from the Falklands to Bristol and, no doubt in gratitude for his generosity towards the old iron ship, its trustees were quick to give their blessing to our use of the name.

The day of the launch was beautiful. The weather was beautiful, the lady guests were beautiful, and so were the good folk of Ramsgate and the thousands of schoolchildren who lined the quay and waved their Union Jacks to greet the Princess. It was a fairy-tale day as her helicopter whirred down from a clear blue sky. The Parachute Brigade formed a Guard of Honour and the Regimental Band played as she was greeted by Lord Astor, Jack Hayward, and myself. We introduced Maureen and several other V.I.P.s to Her Royal Highness and then Samantha, looking fabulous in clan tartan outfit, presented her with a bouquet.

The world's Press and television were there recording yet another Red Letter Day in the Blyth life. With grace and poise Princess Anne launched *Great Britain II,* christening her with a bottle of Moussec, chosen because we had an all-British boat and we wanted to launch her with a British drink that was as near to champagne as possible. The bottle broke, there was that heart-stopping moment when nothing moved, then slowly *Great Britain II* made her stately passage into the water for the first time. It was a tremendous moment.

Three friends, Chris Waddington, Phil Wolfinden and Don Blewitt, were on board and quickly the yacht was tied up alongside the quay. The Princess, Jack and I walked through the cheering crowds for a tour of inspection on board. Actually, to describe it as a tour is something of an exaggeration because beauty with *Great Britain II* that day was very much skin deep. It was like one of those Hollywood film sets of Main Street, looking great from the outside but really nothing but a shell. International Paints had once again done a great paint job and the hull and deck looked fine, but below was chaos. Bits of wood, workmen's tools, unconnected instruments, it was terrible. So when the Princess asked what it was like below I quaked. It was one of those situations where truth is the only solution.

"Sorry Ma'am," I said. "It is in an awful state. We haven't even got any ladders for you to go down." The Princess laughed and so I continued. "I must apologise and perhaps I could make up in part for the diminished tour by asking you to come back when the fitting out is complete.

The crew and I would be deeply honoured if you could come for a sail with us."

"I would be delighted to come," said the Princess and to me it meant more than all the ballyhoo that had gone on for the previous hour. It signified to me that the launch was more than just another engagement as far as she was concerned. She was keen enough to want to come sailing with us.

I asked if she would object to my mentioning her proposed sail when I made my speech at the champagne reception Jack Hayward gave after the launch. She said she did not mind, but in the end I forebore from announcing it because we decided to keep the visit as private as possible. I felt that everyone including the Princess would enjoy the sail so much more and as events turned out I did exactly the right thing.

The day after the launching I wrote to Buckingham Palace asking the Princess if she could suggest a date in July when she could join us for a sail and emphasising that we would keep the visit strictly private. Back came the reply—by return of course—that August 1st would be a suitable date and so began a fever of activity to complete the fitting out and to get everything shipshape.

There was added excitement when, a couple of days before the sail, we received a letter from the Palace asking if it would be all right if Captain Mark Phillips came along too. This was just after the confirmation of their romance had been announced so for us it was tremendous.

We went through agonies to keep the whole thing secret in order that there would be no Press and so guarded were the crew that many of them did not even tell their close relatives.

On the appointed day we all assembled beside the pontoon at the Royal Southern Yacht Club. There was the crew, Jack and his daughter Susan, Chris Waddington, Terry Bond, and me. Then just like in the story books along came a maroon Reliant Scimitar with Mark Phillips being driven by Princess Anne and the ever-present detective with his knees up to his nose—there is very little room in the back of a Scimitar—and a couple of dogs to keep him company.

The Princess looked fabulous. Usually I am not observant when it comes to women's clothes but I have no trouble in recalling what Princess Anne wore that day. She had on black cord Levi's, a light cotton blouse, and a pair of yachting shoes. Her hair was pulled back in a pony tail and she was perfectly kitted for sailing. Captain Phillips wore similarly casual clothes and carried that cap that has almost become his trademark. We had a memorable sail. Princess Anne has a knack of making one feel perfectly at ease, and the ice was quickly broken as we sailed away from the pontoon when crewman Mike Thompson said to Captain Phillips: "You will get very bored sitting in the cockpit, Sir. Come for'ard with me." When they reached the mast Mike gave him a halliard.

"Now, Sir, when I tell you just pull this and the sail will go up," said Mike.

Captain Phillips is no doubt a fine soldier but when it comes to sailing he is something of a learner so when Mike told him to pull he pulled. What the awful Mike had not told him was that it takes three men to hoist that sail so by the time it was halfway up the mast the Phillips' muscles were straining more than somewhat. However, he took the whole thing in good part, which was a good job because he is a big man and Mike could well have found himself swimming back to Portsmouth.

On the other hand, Princess Anne is a remarkably fine sailor. After our salad lunch—I had asked my sister Edie to prepare it at her Portsmouth home because I had not yet learned to trust the culinary capabilities of the crew—the Princess took the wheel. She steered well and held a steady course. In a moment of crisis she demonstrated just how useful she could be on a boat. The inner foresail sheet caught on a winch and the Princess jumped from the cockpit to the deck and released it before any of the crew could move. It was an example of natural seamanship that proved that the Princess has inherited her father's love of the sea.

Exercise Dry Sail at Hawick where the crew selection took place

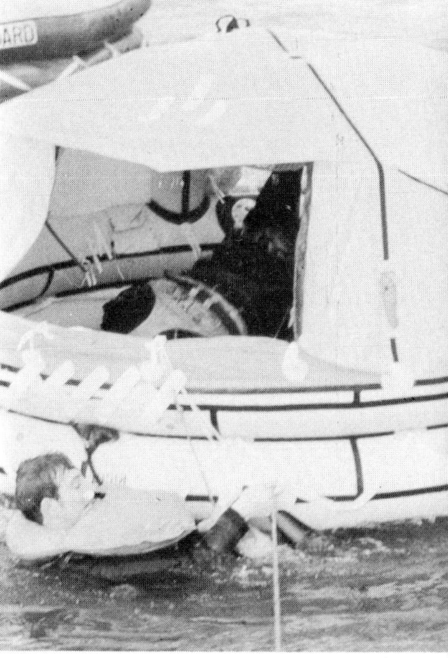

Iore training at the Sea Survival School

Laying the fibreglass and fitting the bulkheads. The paras themselves helped finish the boat in their own time at the yard in Sandwich

The boat and her crew: front row, l. to r. Brian Daniels, Alec Honey, Chay Blyth, Mike Thompson; middle row, l. to r. Len Price, Robbie Robertson, John Rist, Eric Blunn, Alan Toone, Peter Bates; back row, l. to r. Rod Fisher (reserve), Eddie Hope, Bernie Hosking

below left, the author with Jack Hayward; right, Alan Gurney, the designer

John Rist at the helm

The spinnaker wrapped round the backstay. Cookie and Len are aloft sorting things out.

Robbie and Bernie, back to camera. The boom can be seen bending; a few days later it broke and washed Bernie overboard

The broken boom being repaired

Some of the opposition: above *Pen Duick VI,* with its uranium hull, an extreme in ocean racers; below, *Adventure,* the Navy's boat, anti-fouling in Cape Town

Above, Ramon Carlin's *Sayula II,* the winner on handicap; below, *Burton Cutter,* the biggest yacht in the race

The start at Cape Town

Eddie's broken arm comes in for some enthusiastic amateur attention

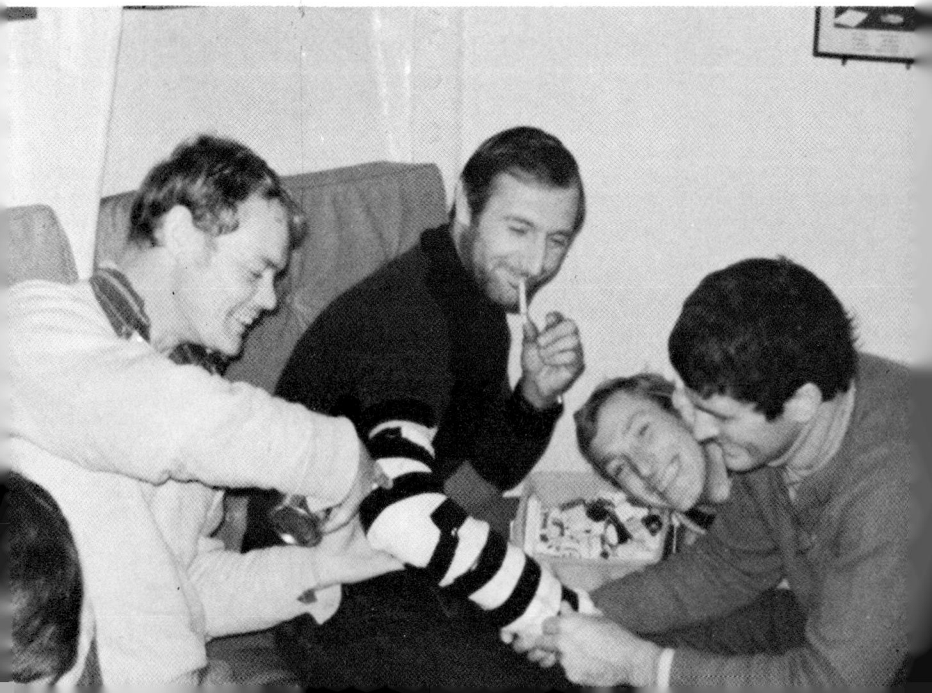

After several hours of great sailing the Princess and Captain Phillips left by high speed launch and the crew took *Great Britain II* back to Portsmouth. That evening Jack threw a "bon voyage" dinner at the Havant Albany for the crew and their wives or girl friends. It was the perfect climax to a perfect day.

Everything had gone according to plan and, most important as far as I was concerned, the crew had not made any obvious *faux pas*. Although they had worked for weeks building the boat, they had had virtually no opportunity to sail in her and they acquitted themselves very well indeed. It would not however be fair to give them all the credit because the man in charge of our sailing activities that day, Chris Waddington, ruled the boat with an air of quiet authority that typifies the man. I seem to have known Chris and his wife Ruth for most of my life so I can vouch with confidence that he is a fine sailor. Although we have long and often heated arguments he has taught me a great deal about the sea.

I was proud too of how smart the crew had been. They all had regulation Army haircuts, so much more presentable than the lanky shoulder-length locks which turn men into women nowadays. We all wore eye-catching orange jumpers given to us by Lyle and Scott, we had bought dark blue shirts and we wore similar matching trousers. Initially we had wanted light blue trousers but our search along the clothing shops of the South Coast had proved to be in vain.

Eventually Terry Bond went to a store in his home town, Wolverhampton, and after a lot of telephone calls to their branches they managed to locate fourteen pairs of trousers with the right waist and inside leg measurements and in just the right shade of blue. He drove them all the way from Staffordshire to Chris Waddington's boatyard at Portchester, near Portsmouth, where *Great Britain II* was berthed. There was a smug smile on his face as he handed over the slacks because he had succeeded in locating the garments where we had failed. The smile turned rather sickly as he drove them all the way back to Wolverhampton again. The waist and leg measurements had been fine but they do not make trousers with burly paratroopers in mind and seams shattered as big thighs and rumps tried to squeeze into them. Eventually we settled for conventional dark grey.

* * *

Slowly the completion of the boat came nearer but I now had a new worry. With only a few weeks to go to the start of the race, the crew were still working on the finishing off of the yacht while they should really have been gaining sailing experience. The strenuous building work was keeping them physically fit and they were so wrapped up in the project that they had devoured the theoretical work with enthusiasm, yet their knowledge of the sea and its unpredictability was still sparse. Because of personal problems, our sixteen men of the cottage were now down to fourteen, and I knew that because of weight considerations, I would have to whittle the number down still further. Before making such decisions it was vital that I saw the men in sailing action, because an incident during our early training had taught me that one cannot be sure of the reactions of any man.

We were on a Sea Survival Course at HMS *Mountbatten*. It followed immediately on a week-long dinghy sailing course we had attended at the National Sailing Centre at Cowes and I was feeling fairly pleased with the way the men had coped with their first taste of life on salt water. We had expected that the survival course would be tough and we were not disappointed. The course was vitally important because it was teaching us what to do in time of trouble. Most yachtsmen have fortunately never had to struggle out of a strong sea into a dinghy wearing survival kit, but after our experience that week the crew of *Great Britain II* can state that it is very difficult and quite frightening.

We had two life rafts on the survival test, with my Number Two, Captain Alec Honey, in charge of one and me overseeing the other. There were seven men in each boat. The sea was choppy and the life rafts did not exactly inspire confidence. We had to carry out various exercises like bailing out, pumping up where necessary, and so on. One of the men in my dinghy just sat there and refused to move. When I told him to get off his fat backside and help the others he just stared stonily at me. He was petrified, incapable of carrying out an order or thinking clearly. When we got back to land I had to tell him that he was of no further use as a crew member.

I do not blame the man concerned and I certainly would not call him a coward. In Scotland he had been among the best of the chaps and he had passed the dinghy course with flying colours. But the moment he stepped into the rubber dinghy fear took over and there was little or nothing he could do about it. Some folk have a fear of heights, others are terror-stricken when they see a spider, grown men sweat with fright if they have to go into the confined space of a lift. We all have a fear factor built into us and luckily one crew member discovered his before we sailed.

Although time was critical and I often felt that we would not make the start line, I knew subconsciously that we would succeed in the end because we had so much good-will and enthusiasm behind us. Firms and individuals were inspired with Great Britain fever to devote energy and expertise to our cause. To mention them all by name would take up the rest of the book so I will content myself with a few words about just one of them, a man typical of a score who helped us during these last frantic days. John Wright is his name, a Derbyshire engineer whose company goes back to his grandfather's day. I first met him in 1972 when I went to Burton-on-Trent to open a motor rally for the Royal National Lifeboat Institution. John was the organiser and told me that a part of his business was making fuel and water tanks for boats. I tend to store such snippets of information almost subconsciously, so when it was time to commission the water tanks I remembered John and telephoned him. Not only did he make the tanks for a fraction of the cost that I would normally have expected to pay, he also did many other excellent engineering jobs for the yacht. He made the hatches and he designed and built the inner forestay release lever, which worked perfectly and saved us hours of toil.

Without John and Chris Waddington and men like them *Great Britain II* would never have been built.

There were two personal accidents during these final stages of building that I was going to have cause to remember and regret. Eddie Hope, travelling to pick up a piece of equipment, had a car smash and the damage to his arm resulted in the insertion of a steel plate. Little did we realise at the time just how serious that accident was going to prove. The other accident was to Bernie Hosking, who fell from a loft while carrying a heavy piece of equipment. He was taken to hospital suffering from concussion. No one can be quite sure how serious a bang on the head can be, so naturally we were all delighted when the doctors declared Bernie completely fit.

* * *

With just a week to go I knew precisely the men who would be my companions for the next eight months, the men who would crew *Great Britain II* for better or for worse. As a final check I asked the friend of a friend, a very well known lady psychologist in Glasgow, to test our compatibility and to assess how individuals would cope with the voyage. We each filled out a long series of question-and-answer forms.

Her report, which was completely confidential and was read only by me, makes interesting reading.

> It is not usual for a psychologist to interpret test material X without personal knowledge of the individuals concerned and an opportunity to explore

in an interview some of the issues raised by the results. In this instance the task of individual interpretation falls upon you!

There were some difficulties associated with the test scores so there is nothing particularly absolute about them. However, the sort of things that the test measured were as follows:

EXTRAVERSION

Someone with a high 'E' has a positive need/hunger for variety—scenery, people, food—many aspects of life. They seek the stimulation of new situations and extreme situations which arouse them and waken them up, for example, plenty of noise. They tend to smoke more. They crave excitement, take chances, often stick their necks out, act on the spur of the moment and are generally impulsive individuals preferring action to planning and thought.

They are also superficially gregarious people who tend to have a lot of acquaintances.

People high on Extraversion exercise relatively less control over the expression of their feelings. For example they become angry very easily and subside again quickly.

It has been shown also that people high on Extraversion have a *lower* capacity for enduring or persevering in a task and particularly for tolerating boredom. There is also some evidence that they are *slightly* less able to tolerate pain and physical privation.

People low on Extraversion are the mirror image of what has been described above. They are high on perseverance and self-control, cautious in taking decisions and acting, and well able to tolerate loneliness and boredom.

NEUROTICISM

People high on Neuroticism tend to over-react to events, they develop anxiety easily and they maintain

> high levels of anxiety longer than those with low Neuroticism score. (Those with low 'N' score will find that anxiety drops quicker after an anxiety-producing event).
>
> This over-reacting is an inborn constitutional thing and bears no relation to courage or cowardice. It is something which the person learns to cope with or not to cope with as the case may be.
>
> It is possible that people with low 'N' scores are just lacking in imagination or even that they might fail to be alarmed when they should be. Low 'N' scores are less able to tolerate pain.

After that explanation of 'E' and 'N' the psychologist commented:

> In general the personality pattern which theoretically would best fit a long and perhaps sometimes boring voyage around the world, under conditions of deprivation, would be someone with a low 'E' score and a low 'N' score.
>
> But paradoxically enough these people are in fact the least likely to be attracted by the idea. Perhaps this explains in part why none of the crew tested produced this sort of profile.
>
> On the other hand, somebody with an extremely high score on both 'E' and 'N' together should be regarded with particular caution, as possessing a potentially explosive combination of personality traits in the sort of situation you have in mind.

I had already decided who would be in the crew and I reckoned that I knew my men. Nevertheless it transpired that the psychologist's report showed a remarkable insight into the individual and as I list the crew I will indicate the psychologist's assessment.

CHAY BLYTH. Ex-sergeant. Born Hawick, Scotland,

1941. Married. Experienced ocean sailor. Skipper and navigator on *Great Britain II.* Very high 'E', between average and high 'N'.

ALEC HONEY. Captain. Born Working 1942. Married. Some sailing experience. Number One and Watch Officer. High 'E', very low 'N'.

MIKE THOMPSON. Sergeant. Born Flintshire 1945. Married. Some sailing experience. Number Two and Bosun. Very high 'E', average 'N'.

BRIAN DANIELS. Captain. Born Dulwich 1932. Married. Engineer and winchman. No previous sailing experience. High 'E', average 'N'.

BERNIE HOSKING. Private. Born Berkhamsted 1947. Single. No sailing experience. Rigger/foredeck. Low 'E', high 'N'.

LEN PRICE. Lance corporal. Born Driffield 1945. Single. V. experienced sailor. Rigger/helmsman. Average 'E', average 'N'.

ERIC BLUNN. Private. Born Stockton on Tees 1946. Married. No sailing experience. Plumber/helmsman. High 'E', low 'N'.

JOHN RIST. Private. Born Brighton 1950. Single. No sailing experience. Sailmaker/mainsheet. Very high 'E', between average and high 'N'.

PETER BATES. Corporal. Born Andover 1948. Single. No sailing experience. Sailmaker/foredeck. High 'E', average 'N'.

ROBBIE ROBERTSON. Corporal. Born Chelmsford 1944. Married. Experienced sailor. Shipwright/foredeck. Very high 'E', high 'N'.

ALAN TOONE. Private. Born Croydon 1947. Married. Cook/bosun's assistant/medic/winchman. No previous sailing experience. High 'E', low 'N'.

EDDIE HOPE. Lance Sergeant. Born Berwick-on-Tweed 1945. Married. Dinghy sailor. Medic/foredeck. Not assessed by psychologist because he was in hospital with a broken arm when the tests were done.

That was the team and the psychologist's comments. At the end of her report she classed as "doubtful" Robbie Robertson (because of the combination of a very high 'E' and a high 'N') and Bernie Hosking (because of his high 'N' score). She also classed as "doubtful but rather less so" John Rist and Chay Blyth.

5

Buckingham Palace

Offshore racing has become enormously popular and there is now a respectable body of experience in this sort of seamanship. At the same time some intrepid navigators have pioneered the really long distance passages, frequently single handed. The Royal Naval Sailing Association and Whitbreads have put these two circumstances together and organised an offshore race on a grand scale. The Round-the-World Race is a challenge in a new dimension to all those who are looking for something more demanding than the conventional passage races.

All sorts of surprising and unexpected things are bound to happen and I am sure the Race Committee will have to give decisions on some very original problems. However, I have little doubt that it will be a great success—particularly for those who finish.

Philip
Admiral
Royal Navy Sailing Association

That was the message sent to the Race Organising Committee by the Duke of Edinburgh to launch the race as, at the start of September 1973, eighteen boats turned up at HMS *Vernon,* Portsmouth, to compete in the most remarkable sea competition the world has ever seen.

The race was to be organised by the Royal Navy Sailing Association, assisted by the Royal Navy and Royal Albert Yacht Club, the Cruising Association of South Africa, the Cruising Yacht Club of Australia and the Iate Clube de Rio de Janeiro. There were some very impressive names among the list of officials involved in the organisation, including Rear Admiral Otto Steiner, the chairman of the Race Committee, who was to prove a fine overseer of the whole event.

Considering that a crewed race of this length had never been contemplated before the rules were remarkably well drawn up and easy to follow as far as competitors were concerned.

Every yacht would sail under current International Yacht Racing Union rules and to qualify as competitors they had to (a) have a valid IOR rating of not less than 33 feet and not more than 70 feet (b) be single hulled and (c) conform to the Safety Regulations laid down. The minimum crew to be carried was five and the use of automatic steering by mechanical or electrical means or by wind vanes was prohibited.

When we arrived at HMS *Vernon,* the yacht was inspected to ensure that we complied with the safety rules laid down for the race. In addition to those stipulated by the Offshore Racing Council, these included additional water storage, a minimum of two life saving rafts able to carry the whole crew, additional fire extinguishers and radio transmitters and receivers. Included in the compulsory navigational equipment were marine compasses, charts, sextant, accurate time piece, radio direction finder, lead line or echo sounder, log or speedometer and navigation lights. In addition electronic wind speed and direction indicators could be fitted.

The plan was to start on September 8th from Southsea

and sail to Cape Town. The organisers were fairly flexible about the restart and we were told it would be about ten days to a fortnight after the second yacht had docked in South Africa. The same situation would apply for the start of the third leg from Sydney but the start of the final leg from Rio back to Portsmouth would be staggered so that in theory all the boats would arrive back at about the same time.

Stops could be made without penalty at any port on the globe. Crewmen who were injured or unwell could be put ashore and provisions could be taken on board but no new crew members could be added to the yacht except at the three scheduled stopping ports.

The handicapping system is rather difficult for the layman to understand. First of all the yachts are measured, not just their length but also width, sails, angle of heel, and dozens of other points. These facts are fed into a computer and comparative handicaps are produced. *Great Britain II* emerged as the "Scratch" boat, which means that as far as the Corrected Time situation was concerned we had to give time to every other competitor.

I suppose the nearest comparision would be to golf, where each player is handicapped according to his abilities. If everyone played precisely to his handicap all the players would finish with the same net score. In the yacht race, if all the yachts performed as the committee assessed they would (in an eight month round-the-world competition it seemed rather a vain hope) on Corrected Time they would all finish at precisely the same moment. Continuing the golf analogy Corrected Time was equivalent to the handicap prize and Elapsed Time was the same as the overall Club Championship for the best player with the lowest actual score.

Because we had not had time to do the maximum trials, we would not do well with the handicapping system, so we were going all out for the Elapsed Time Prize. We were going to be the yacht that had sailed round the world fastest.

The first leg to Cape Town is 7090 miles and, allowing for the slower boats, the organisers expected the restart there to be about the first week of November. Sydney was another 6550 miles and we anticipated leaving there on the 8370 mile trip to Rio just before Christmas. The home run from South America is 5560 miles and informed guesses put our departure date around the last week in February.

The yachts were handicapped on a time-on-distance basis and I was not surprised to see that *Great Britain II* was the scratch yacht. For the handicap prize we were going to have to concede time to every other competitor and as I looked around the basin at HMS *Vernon,* I realised that my ambitions of sweeping the prize board were pretty hopeless. We had been heavily handicapped and even in such a long race the advantages the handicapping system gave my rivals were formidable.

However, when I first embarked on the project I had determined that if there was going to be a race around the world then I wanted to skipper the fastest yacht in it. *Great Britain II* had been designed to sail round the globe in fewer days than any other yacht and if we lifted that prize I would be more than satisfied.

It was only when I looked closely at the other yachts that I realised just how strong the competition was. One boat, Eric Tabarly's *Pen Duick VI,* was awesome to me.

While *Great Britain II* had been berthed in Wicor Marine we had received a visit from Eric Tabarly. We were flattered and at the same time apprehensive because this was scrutiny by the most professional of them all.

He is a man of few words and as I showed him over the yacht he made little comment. Back on shore he said in his quiet accent: "You have a great boat, Chay. Like *Pen Duick*, it is untried. I am looking forward to racing against you."

Now at Portsmouth I had a chance to see Eric's yacht. He invited me on board and I stepped on to a racing machine where strength appeared to be everything. My eye was particularly taken by the big winches, special productions for this fabulous yacht. *Pen Duick* did not have the smoothness of *Great Britain II* but her enormous power was obvious. Without appearing to be too nosey I inspected every detail of that boat and when I got back I told our crew:

"She is a superb yacht. We've really got something to beat. My only criticism is that in my opinion her standing rigging is too small and I was surprised to see that her mast is stepped on the deck."

I regarded *Sayula* too as a major threat. The pre-publicity gave the impression that Ramon Carlin was approaching the event more as a pleasure cruise than anything else, but one glance at *Sayula* dispelled any such thoughts. Here was a superb yacht crewed by a team of real professionals. Ramon had chosen his men carefully and all the skills needed to sail around the world were there.

Grand Louis too was a proven schooner that had done the Fastnet Race and was in with a good chance and *33 Export*—she used to be called *Ralph* and did well in a Transatlantic Race—was a force to be reckoned with.

Adventure was a Nicholson 55 with a team from the Royal Navy and, as I had said in a television interview a few days earlier, production boats may do better initially than "one-off" boats because all their shortcomings had been discovered and ironed out before the start of the race. Obviously, the Navy were going to make every effort.

The other yacht that I considered a danger to our chances was *Burton Cutter*. Built of aluminium she was a giant 84 feet long, and her skipper, Les Williams was one of the most experienced ocean racing yachtsmen in Britain. *Burton Cutter* was in a terribly unfinished state below decks, but as every yachtsman knows, it is the sail that pushes the boat along. Les may have had chaos below, but all his sailing equipment and deck gear was in place and in prime working order. And that's what counted. She was ready to sail as long as the deck fittings and sails were in position. Maybe a few fire extinguishers and bunks were missing, but they do not pull the boat through the water.

The rightly respected Editor of *Yachting World,* Bernard Hayman, had the following to say:

> Interest, in Britain at any rate, inevitably focussed on *Great Britain II.*
>
> She was the great glamour boat, handsome to look at, ruthless by normally accepted standards, and a boat with the magic of Chay Blyth's name associated with her. [Blush, Blush—C.B.]. Alan Gurney, a Briton living and working in U.S.A., is one of the few men in the world with ample experience of the design of boats of this size. She is the most extreme he has yet attempted because, despite her actual displacement of 33 tons, she is really very light indeed; not far removed from an enormous dinghy. Below, she is spartan but except perhaps for a lack of handholds and other personal comforts she is adequate. On deck she is almost barren because the vast size makes the lifelines look almost like toe rails. Generally a well prepared boat but much of the gear seemed only just strong enough.
>
> In contrast *Pen Duick VI,* the other big glamour boat in the race, gave the impression of such incredible strength that it was hard to consider these two boats in the same breath. Part of this visual contrast is because (as a generalisation) *Great Britain* has stainless steel fittings and *Pen Duick* aluminium ones and the light alloy fitting has to be two or three times as bulky to give equivalent strength. But the fact remains that *Pen Duick* looks as though she could be broached in the Roaring Forties and still come up smiling. *Great Britain II* may be ruthless but *Pen Duick VI* is pioneering a new type of boat. There can never have been any pretence that she was a gentleman's yacht used for racing. She is a machine and beautiful, only in the sense that say a Land Rover might be admired, because it does its job. *Pen Duick VI* is a comparatively ugly boat but one which takes one's breath away. Having once abandoned any sort of coachroof, skylight or normal comforts the

> deck becomes one large working cockpit with pedestals for winches where necessary and recesses for men to work where necessary. Vital racing accessories, like kicking straps, are no longer angled-spans as in a dinghy, or hastily (and temporarily) arranged purchases to the rail, as in most large offshore racing boats. The full width of the deck for both main and mizzen is swept with radiused tracks and they look strong enough to lift the whole boat!

As usual Bernard Hayman was right. *Pen Duick VI* was a 74 foot formidable ketch, a machine built specially for the race and skippered by the greatest ocean racing sailor ever. As I looked at her matt black hull I had every reason to be pensive. Before the race the bookies were offering 6–1 against *Great Britain II* and 8–1 against *Pen Duick VI,* and I was tempted to have a few bob on Tabarly.

The biggest boat in the race was *Burton Cutter,* whose name had just been changed from *Windward Spirit* as a tribute to a last minute sponsor. Her length overall was 84 feet, a ketch skippered by her joint owner, Leslie Williams. Les is a good friend and a great character as well as being a fine ocean seaman. His boat was designed by John Sharp and built in aluminium and was perhaps the least tried of all the entries. A week before the start the very experienced crew were still working on standing rigging and basic ballasting problems. A lesser man than Les would have withdrawn from the mass start but he just carried on at his usual seemingly-unhurried pace and confounded all the critics by arriving in South Africa before anyone else!

Another private British entry was *Second Life,* a 71 foot ketch skippered by Roddy Ainslie. She is an Ocean 71 design and her crew had paid £3,000 each for the privilege of taking part in the race. One of the crew was to have been Roddy's wife Sue, but a few days before the start she discovered that she was pregnant and so rightly decided that a bumpy trip around the world was no place for a growing embryo.

There were two official Services entries to complete the British line up. *Adventure* was the Nicholson 55 entered by the Royal Navy, a cutter that had done many thousands of sailing miles in her warm up for the race. She was to be manned by four separate crews on the different legs of the race, and the personnel were to be from the Navy, the Marines, and the Air Force. *British Soldier* was the Army's entry and they too planned to change crews at the stopping ports.

Besides *Pen Duick VI* there were three French entries. *33 Export* was a 57 foot yawl entered by Dominique Guillet and Jean-Pierre Millet; *Grand Louis* was a schooner, 61 feet overall, owned and skippered by Andre Viant; *Kriter* was a 68 foot ketch sponsored by a wine company and skippered by Jack Grout.

The Italians had three yachts. *CS e RB* was a 50 foot ketch designed by Robert Clark and skippered by Doi Malingri. *Guia* was one of the smallest boats in the race, a 45 foot sloop owned and skippered by Georgio Falck. *Tauranga* was a Swan 55 foot yawl with Eric Pascoli as her captain.

From Poland came another small boat, *Copernicus,* which had been specially designed and built in mahogany for the race. This ketch was skippered by Zygfryd Perlicki. Also from Poland came a 55 foot 13-year-old ketch, *Otago,* built in steel and captained by Zdzislaw Pienkawa.

Jakaranda was a South African entry, a former Admiral's Cup sloop measuring 56 feet overall and skippered by John Goodwin.

Sayula II was owned and entered by the Mexican washing machine millionaire Ramon Carlin. It was a Swan 65 ketch designed by Sparkman and Stephens.

Completing the line up was a remarkable old German boat, *Peter von Danzig*. Built in 1936 this steel yawl skippered by Achim Meyer and Reinhard Laucht already had six Atlantic crossings to her credit.

They were a motley collection of yachts with two things in common. They were manned by determined crews and they were setting out on the most fascinating race of the century.

The writing and reading of ship's logs can become very boring, particularly when the same mind is recording happenings day after day. Therefore the story of the voyage on the following pages is recorded not only by me but by two of my crew, John Rist and Eric Blunn. Personally I found reading their logs afterwards a fascinating exercise. To compare their reactions, the priorities they placed on events gave me a fresh insight into the trip.

Our thoughts were constantly with our families and friends back home and we derived great comfort from the fact that Captain John Williams D.C.M. of the 16th Parachute Brigade took it on himself to keep our relatives informed of our progress via a regular "Lonely Hearts Newsletter".

PART TWO

Portsmouth—Cape Town

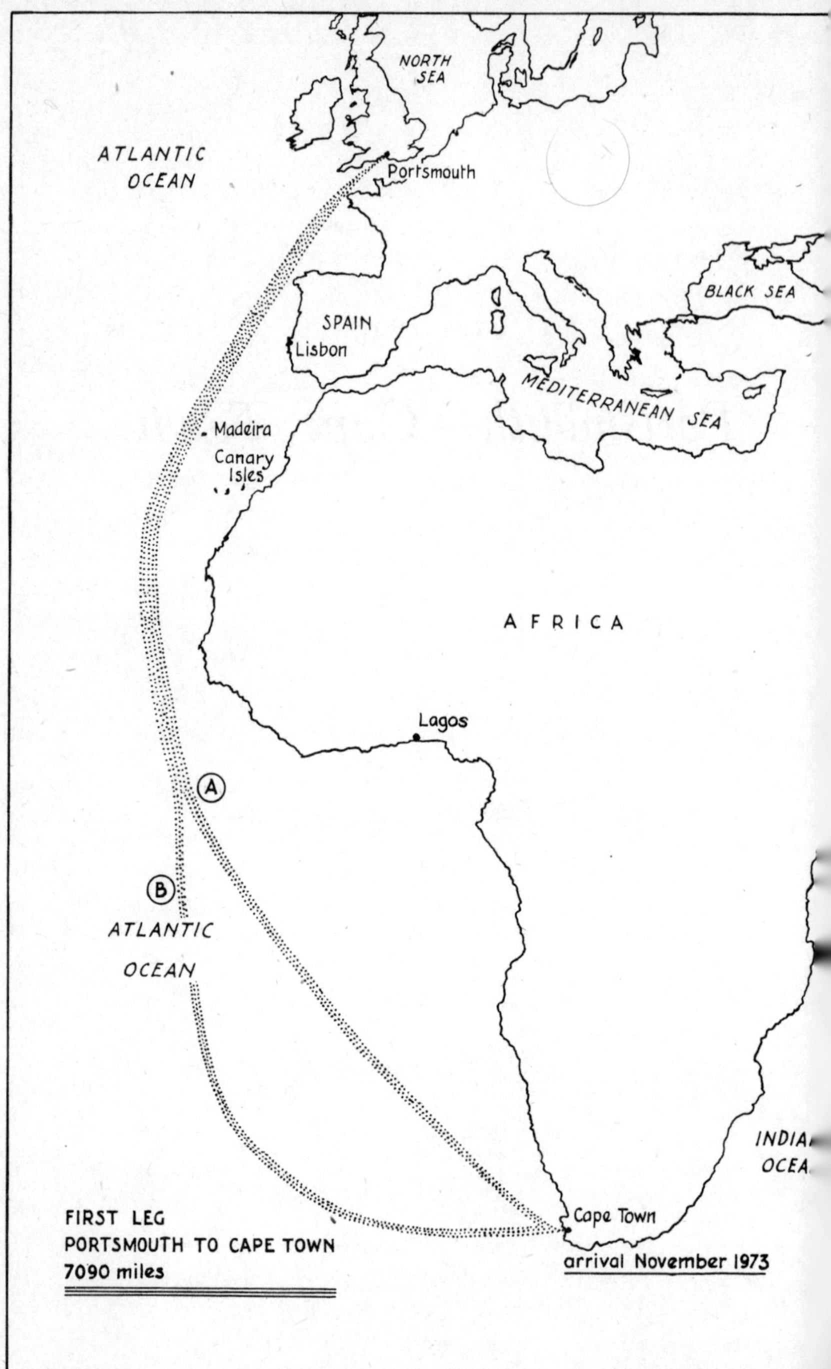

A The yachts, like *Burton Cutter*, *Adventure* and *Second Life*, who risked the high pressure in the South Atlantic had better luck than those like *Sayula II*, *Great Britain II*, *33 Export* and *Pen Duick IV*, who were becalmed when they took the southern route to sail round it.

B At this point *Pen Duick VI* had to limp to Rio with a broken mast.

6

Saturday, September 8th (Chay Blyth) DAY ONE.

The day started very early. I awoke at 06.15 to shower and wash my hair. When you are leaving home for eight months there is always a hell of a lot to do. Surprisingly, when we arrived at the yacht there was a pleasant and restful calm atmosphere—we were as ready as we would ever be. Only I seemed to be restless, pacing backwards and forwards checking and double checking that we had everything.

Poor Maureen and Samantha. I had little time for them. I looked at Maureen and she smiled knowingly, meaning that I should concentrate on the boat because they would be all right. Around us the crew were saying goodbye to their wives, girl friends and families. The Brigadier was chatting with Chris Waddington. John Rist had his arm around his girl friend, Sandra. I hate these last goodbyes.

I looked at my watch. 10.00 B.S.T. "OK, that's it," I shouted "Let's go." I wanted to get out there an hour beforehand to do some timed starts so that we would go over the line seconds after the gun.

As I kissed and hugged Maureen she pressed a cross into my hand; she has always given me one when I leave on an adventure.

We motored out to the start line then I cut the engine and just drifted for a while to get the true wind direction and speed. We hoisted sail and sailed back and forth from the mouth of Spit Elbow over the line. When we had done this three times the start line was getting so congested with other competitors and literally thousands of sightseers that I sailed away in order to avoid a collision. There was plenty of time and I looked around for Jim Alabaster from Ratsey and Lapthorn. We had not received our starcut spinnaker and Jim had promised to deliver it before we crossed the start line. Sure enough, as I looked out for him, a speedboat came alongside and Jim transferred the spinnaker. Talk about last minute jobs!

The start line was chaos. Big ships, little ships—even one yacht anchored. We had planned to come from weather and now was the time. The countdown gun had been fired and our stop watch started. "Ready about," I shouted. "We're going for the line." We tacked. Len Price was on the helm. Pete Bates watching out and the rest of the crew at stations.

Round we went and I looked for Tabarly but I couldn't see him. I checked the transit marks and sailed along but not over them. Suddenly Tabarly was beside us but to leeward and that I did not mind. *British Soldier* was further to leeward. We sailed together, *Great Britain II* and *Pen Duick VI,* and it must have been quite a sight. Ten seconds, nine seconds, eight seconds, Alec counted down for Len. BANG! We shot over the line. I am sure we were first over, but Tarbarly was close on our heels.

I couldn't believe my eyes. Straight across our path lay *Vendredi, 13*—128 feet of useless yacht. I was flabbergasted. Pete called for him to move but if anything he moved more in our way. Apparently it was some stupid French television crew intent on getting good pictures.

I hailed Eric Tabarly for more room. He bore off and we went through, *GB II* one side *PD VI* the other. So close did we come that Eric and Eddie were able to grab *Vendredi's* rigging to fend us off.

Once clear, the two yachts were neck and neck but we inched our way forward and then took his wind and drew ahead. It was very exciting and gradually we increased our lead to about a quarter of a mile.

Alec Honey was navigating and he shouted from below, "You'll have to tack." I couldn't understand that. Why should we have to tack so soon? I jumped down to check for myself and sure enough Alec's workings seemed right. I went on deck to get ready and then I noticed it. Len had put his camera down by the compass. It had batteries and cells and sure enough when I moved the camera the compass swung round to give us a new heading. Len and I exchanged glances but no words were spoken. He was obviously very sorry.

We raced from Bembridge Buoy and I gave Pete the binoculars to look for it. Eventually he spotted the buoy and the tide was setting us past it. I asked Len to pinch and try to make ground. "It's no good skipper," he warned me at least a dozen times. "We're not going to make it." If we could round the buoy without tacking we would gain even further on Eric. I looked at the buoy and Tabarly and with blind faith I decided not to tack. We got right up to the buoy and we must have been five feet or even less from it. I yelled to Len to bear away but it was no go. The yacht stopped dead and as yachtsmen know—"At all times keep steerage way". It was hopeless. For a good five minutes we had the jib all over the place before we eventually got under way again. Meanwhile of course Eric had tacked and was leaving us astern.

The next horlicks came when we hoisted the starcut spinnaker. The ties were too strong and it was hard breaking it open. Finally we got it up and we were off again. All this messing about meant that the rest of the fleet had almost caught us up but we started to pull away again. Just before dark we could see *Pen Duick* ahead. I guessed he was about two miles in front and with 6,700 miles to go that's not much of an advantage.

Same Day (John Rist).

The big day has come at last. There were times when I thought I would never make it. Sandra stayed the night with my family and we all made an early start to arrive at HMS *Vernon* at 08.30. I showed everyone around the boat. It was the first time they had seen it and they were quite impressed. The rest of the crew began to arrive and I think we were all a little bit nervous. When the time came for us to sail out into the Solent I felt a bit sad saying goodbye to my parents. I purposely said goodbye to Sandra last of all. I am going to miss her a hell of a lot.

What a sight out in the Solent! I have never seen so many boats in all my life. We made a text book start with ourselves and Tabarly crossing the line together.

We made a bad mistake at Bembridge Buoy. The tide was pushing us down and we had to tack to go round it. *Pen Duick* got around first time and took the lead. We lost her at night in the fog. We experienced our first real disaster tonight when we were hit by a sudden squall and blew out the light spinnaker. Plenty of sewing in the morning no doubt!

For the first few days we were plagued by fog and poor winds. The light spinnaker that John referred to blew because of the crew's inexperience, the squall hit us and we just did not get it down fast enough. The watch responsible were upset particularly because it was a most important sail. I noticed that everyone was on edge and it was undoubtedly due to the fog. I kept reassuring them that being fogbound was perfectly safe, because my theory is that other ships will pick up a yacht with a radar reflector. In fog they will be using radar, whereas in good weather they rely purely on visibility. It is a good theory but I am not sure whether I truly believe it. In those early days I relied heavily on Mike, Len, and Alec because they had experience.

Wednesday September 12th (John) DAY FIVE
Day's run: 144 miles.

> Quite a blow now with heavy seas at last. So much for the gin-and-tonics and the deckchairs we all expected. We are finding it quite difficult to hoist new headsails with this wind and the movement of the boat. At one time we had the No. 2 Genoa wrapped around the forestay which did not please the skipper very much. As a result of that I spent the rest of the morning repairing a number of small holes in the sails. During the night a gale was blowing and we really had a lot of trouble changing the sails. Eventually we had to put two reefs in the main and we were all absolutely shattered afterwards and soaked to the skin.
>
> We seem to have become accustomed to the two-hours-on two-hours-off watch system and morale is high. I am missing Sandra a lot and wonder what everyone is doing back home. It has not really hit me yet that I will not see her for eight months.

Back home John Williams was sending the first "Lonely Hearts Newsletter" out.

LONELY HEARTS NEWSLETTER NO. 1.
September 13th.

> *Great Britain II* is now well on the way and those of us who are left must settle down for the big wait.
>
> There are all sorts of ways in which we can make the time seem shorter, meeting once a month perhaps? What I would really like to have is ideas, so please drop me a line if you have any and I will pass them on to the others.
>
> The main reason for this first letter is to make sure you have my address and phone number, and to tell you that for news of the race you should tune in to the B.B.C. World Service.

John went on to give the timings of the programmes and to suggest to the wives and girl friends that they kept a diary of day-to-day happenings which he would bring out to us in Cape Town.

Thursday, September 13th (Chay) DAY SIX
Day's run: 187 miles.

> We are having a real run of bad luck. The wind has headed us for three days and this is very unusual for this area. It is coming exactly from the direction we wanted to go. Last night we had heavy squalls. We were down to the No. 4 jib, the No. 2 inner staysail, and two reefs in the mainsail. The No. 3 had a tear in it where it had chafed against the shroud. The worst thing of all is that the lashing holding the jockey pole broke (or came undone) and was lost over the side. It was only by chance that we had brought along a spare.
>
> The chaps were up on the foredeck in our first

real gale. They had their safety harnesses on. Two of them, Alan Toone and Pete Bates, were sick. I take my hat off to Alan; regardless of how he felt he still made us a cup of tea and a snack.

Every time the yacht bangs, up come the impellers. We have tried to lash them down with elastic bungies but they don't seem to work. Now we have piled a coil of rope on each one.

We have ruined our first snatch block. We tried to move the lead further forward, the helmsman luffed up and we got it half in but then he had to bear away and we could not get it out. So now we are minus one block, it is as easy as that.

Friday, September 14th (Chay) DAY SEVEN
Day's run: 189 miles.

These south-west winds have been holding now for four days. It's crazy, we should have following winds. The *Ocean Passages of the World* tells me to stay on the starboard tack and the wind will veer. At the rate we are going we will be in North Africa before that happens. The barometer is rising and I can only hope that it brings a change of wind. I suppose I could tack but then I go almost due west. What a carry on!

I had a telephone call with the *Sunday Times*. My regular contact, Tony Holden, is off on another story so I spoke with John Anderson. It really was wonderful to chat with him again and I knew that our story would be safe because he is one of the great sea writers of all time.

John gave me the positions of some of the other yachts; one surprise was to see how close *Kriter* was.

We've had to put in a tack to the west because of these damned winds. Talk about frustration! It really is most annoying. God knows where the north-east Trades are. I have visions of Tabarly zooming down them while we go back and forth like a bloody yoyo.

Saturday, September 15th (John) DAY EIGHT
Day's run: 166 miles.

We have been at sea now for one week and still we have not found these Trade winds. On the five till seven watch the wind died away almost completely and we were hardly moving. We had a slight cock-up when we managed to get the No. 1 Genoa wrapped around the forestay.

We have a problem with one of our gas bottles; it is leaking but we have been unable to trace it. I also had a minor repair to do on the mizzen staysail because it was chafing along the luff wire.

This afternoon the wind died away again and most of us did a spot of nude sunbathing. A merchant ship came towards us and passed within 200 yards. There was not a single soul on watch—whatever the skipper says I am glad it wasn't foggy. We had a good curry this evening, the only main meal of the day. Breakfast consists of fruit juice, cornflakes, and a hard boiled egg. We have no sugar for our tea and are using sweeteners. It's bloody revolting, I really miss a good cup of Mother's tea. We seem to think and talk a lot about food and as there was not much to do this evening we sat down and started to work out a menu for our first meal in Cape Town.

Sunday, September 16th (Chay) DAY NINE
Day's run: 133 miles.

As predicted today's run was low, just 133 miles. Bernie saw a flying fish last night—we must be near the Trades! The wind is still from west or south-west. It is quite incredible. We have worked out that to get to Cape Town in 40 days we have got to cover 205 miles a day from now on. What a joke, particularly with the Doldrums to go through. I only brought enough food for 40 days so we will have to start reducing on food—that should cause some comment.

I spoke to *Adventure* and *British Soldier* this morning. I am amazed how far *Adventure* is on, and they tell me that *Pen Duick* is only 70 miles ahead of them and to the west. This makes us just about level with Tabarly. I expect to lose this leg of the race to him because of our inexperience but we are determined to give him a good run for his money.

I tried a couple of phone calls to England but they were frustrating. Maureen was out and Jack Hayward's line was so indistinct that we could not hold a conversation.

Everyone on board is settling in well and there have been no clashes so far. Our big problem is boredom when on the wind. Today we had a great clean up and everywhere got washed and wiped down. The yacht looks better for it and I know everyone felt better for the work.

We finished the last of our Bombay ducks, and I for one will miss them.

The next day our luck changed. The wind was kind to us and we broke the 200-miles-a-day barrier for the first time since we had left Portsmouth. At one point we were surfing at over fourteen knots. Communications were better too and I had a long telephone conversation with Maureen. It was our first really good sailing day and John's reactions, recorded here, were typical.

Monday, September 17th (John) DAY TEN
Day's run: 212 miles.

A really great night, we were romping along at 9 knots and had covered 111 miles by seven o'clock this morning. Last night the moon illuminated the sea at about 21.30, we were speeding along and I was fascinated by all the plankton sparkling in the wash of the boat.

My legs are sore as hell after all that sun yesterday. At last the wind has come round and we have the spinnaker up and at times we are doing 13 knots.

It was our first wash day today since leaving U.K. and everyone looks extremely smart. It makes a change because we were all starting to look like out-of-work pirates.

We wash ourselves in salt water and then have two pints of fresh water for a shave and a rinse.

We should now be well clear of Madeira and heading towards the Canaries, then we will be going westwards. The north-east Trades are still with us in force. I hope they keep with us for a week or so. Tonight all hands were called on deck to gybe the spinnaker as it was proving difficult in 20 to 25 knots of wind.

Tuesday, September 18th (Chay) DAY ELEVEN
Day's run: 240 miles.

I will be a gibbering idiot by the time we have finished this trip. We are surfing along at between 12 and 14 knots and of course some of the chaps have not had experience at helming in reasonable seas. We had one or two very very hairy minutes. I could reduce sail but that would not get us to Cape Town fast. I'll take a chance—and pray!

We have topped 15 knots and 240 miles so we have proved that we can travel so long as we have the winds. I take my hat off to the crew—this is their first trip and we are holding Tabarly, the world's best. I honestly will not mind losing this first leg because it is essentially a "getting to know you" period for the men and the boat.

I heard *Adventure* prattling away again. They were calling me but I did not answer, I don't know where they get the power from.

Highlight of the day was the breaking out of a new food pack. It contained some lovely goodies including fruit salad and cream.

Same Day (John).

We have really been moving during the night and have reached 14 knots at times. It is really quite warm and even at night one sweater is enough. We heard *British Soldier* on the radio this morning and so far we are about 250 miles ahead of her; she is still just west of Madeira and we are about 80 miles north of the Canaries. The wind is still blowing hard from the right direction and we have both main and mizzen spinnakers flying. We are really moving and when we get on top of a wave we fly along just like a surfboard. It looks as if the food might improve a bit because we have new rations opened today. There's a rumour going round the boat that we might even get a piece of cake for our mid-morning break.

This afternoon we are still crashing along at 13 to 14 knots. I just hope we can keep this up. We are just north of the Canaries and we are all up on deck soaking up the sun. A few minutes ago we were surfing when suddenly *Great Britain II* dug her bows into a wave, water came pouring in the hatches, and now the deck is covered with sleeping bags out to dry. We actually saw the mountains of Palma a few minutes ago; it will be a long time before we see land again.

Wednesday, September 19th (Chay) DAY TWELVE
Day's run: 191 miles.

First signs of the chaps mumbling. Pete Bates has certainly shown signs of boredom, fed-upness (if that's a word) and apathy. I can't make up my mind whether it is the trip or the fact that he has given up smoking. He has been ratty a couple of times—I overheard him arguing with John—and that is unusual for Pete because he can usually buck a situation quickly and come bounding back. It could be the ciggys but more likely it is the change in our speed. Six and seven knots is very tame when you have been creaming along at 14 knots. I heard *Adventure* give her position. We are 200 miles ahead but really the Navy are doing extraordinarily well. I should think they are well up on handicap.

Bad news about the light spinnaker. John Rist has spent two-and-a-half days fixing it, but 20 minutes after we had hoisted it the bloody thing blew again. Worse still, our sewing machine has packed up. It received a bad bang. We have all had a go at mending it but in vain. This really is bad news.

My next log entry, for Thursday September 20th, has a sad and prophetic ring about it. "Bernie was up to his heroics again today," I wrote. "Instead of winding the spinnaker in to get a heavy sheet on it, Bernie went out to the clew by being hoisted up in the Bosun's Chair and then swinging out. At between 10 and 12 knots that is some feat—you would never have got me to do it."

Meanwhile, back at Aldershot, John Williams was busily mailing his second missive to the wives and girl friends. I only wish I had been able to get hold of a copy—I would probably have understood the handicap ratings better!

LONELY HEARTS NEWSLETTER NO. 2

I expect you will all have been listening to the radio and reading newspaper reports regarding the progress of *Great Britain II* and will therefore know as much as I do about the official race placings.

We are in the leading group of six yachts and all six are very close to each other. In fact a circle of fifty miles would cover all of them, but we have to beat the handicap ratings. This I think requires a little explanation for those who do not understand it. *Great Britain II* was given a scratch handicap which means that the race organisers think we should reach Cape Town first. The remaining yachts all have handicaps and I have noted them below for you.

Great Britain II	—	Scratch
Burton Cutter	—	0.85 of a day
Pen Duick VI	—	1.33 days
Kriter	—	3.83 days
Sayula II	—	4.62 days
Grand Louis	—	5.45 days
33 Export	—	5.52 days
British Soldier	—	5.63 days
Peter von Danzig	—	6.17 days
Otago	—	6.28 days
Adventure	—	6.74 days
Tauranga	—	7.11 days
CS e RB	—	7.79 days
Second Life	—	8.63 days
Guia	—	8.90 days
Copernicus	—	9.33 days

Just to take two examples from the list, if we want to win the first leg on handicap we must reach Cape Town 6.17 days before *Peter von Danzig* and 9.33 days before *Copernicus* and so on.

On top of working out handicaps the yachts are reporting their positions on different days, and the combination of these two factors does not help to give the organisers a true picture of the progress of the race. So do not become downhearted when you hear that we are down the field. The only time we shall be 100% sure is when they reach Cape Town.

After 14 days the yacht has covered 2,396 miles and this is roughly 176 miles a day. The top speed they have achieved is 15½ knots.

Some of you may be a little concerned about all the talk in the newspapers of curry, curry, curry. The only meal that the crew have is the evening meal.

Breakfast, lunch, and tea are made up from fresh or composite rations. The reason for having a curry main meal is that the crew are split into watches and eat at different times. By having curry, which will remain edible for some time, the cook can prepare one meal for both watches.

Friday, September 31st (Chay) DAY FOURTEEN
Day's run: 230 miles.

We had some great laughs this morning. A number of yachts came up on the 09.00 G.M.T. schedule and we contacted *Adventure* to say that we had *Pen Duick's* position and ours, and did they want them? "Yes", came the immediate reply, and I imagined the eager anticipation with which the *Adventure* crew would be waiting to hear the news. After all, we are in a race. Anyway, I gave them two positions, each one on top of a mountain on the Cape Verde Islands. They checked it and had a good laugh but a few minutes later we heard the positions being relayed to other yachts by skippers who had overheard the conversation between ourselves and *Adventure*. It will probably get back to Race Control and I will have a query from them. If so I will tell them that everything is O.K. now because we have kedged off the mountains.

Eddie got a bit upset today. I asked him when he was going on Watch because he was a few minutes late. He shot up on deck snapping: "The Port Watch were late but that was all right, wasn't it?" Unknown to me the Port Watch had been late. Anyway, it obviously upset him because he said he didn't want a cup of tea made for him. I'm afraid food is becoming a major thing with the chaps. I'm surprised. Personally I feel it is an outlet for boredom so I will arrange for us to do more maintenance and clearing up.

Same Day (John).

I worked on sewing the spinnaker all morning and at last got it finished. I hope we never blow another because repairing them is a real gutty job. Still, it's finished and I can look forward to some decent sleep. Bernie caught a flying fish this morning and we had it for a mid-morning snack; it really was very tasty. I have just had a quick check on the cigarette supply and it is getting low. I hope the ciggys last out or I won't have any fingernails left.

The nights are really warm now and we just wear a pair of shorts and a shirt while on watch. The yacht is rolling heavily and it is quite hairy at times because we must be doing about 15 knots and all one can hear is the water rushing along the sides of the hull. We have had a fabulous day's run—230 nautical miles.

Saturday, September 22nd (John) DAY FIFTEEN
Day's run: 227 miles.

We should be about 60 miles east of the Cape Verde Islands by now. The wind dropped during the night so I do not expect we shall be able to break our record for a day's run. There were more sail repairs to do because the regular spinnaker that we had up during the night has got a small hole and a split seam. These small repairs are not too bad but if that other sail blows out again I will go bloody mad.

I think it is going to be another very hot day because the wind has been coming from the African coast. We have been using the light spinnaker and so far, touch wood, it has held. We saw some dolphins this evening and we also had a visitor, a little bird landed on deck. It was absolutely shattered so the skipper grabbed it and took it below. At the moment it is asleep in a cardboard box.

One of our biggest problems was trying to fathom out the race positions. Despite the fact that we had access to several sources—Race Control, the B.B.C. World Service regular reports, weekly chats with Tony Holden at the *Sunday Times,* and almost daily radio conversation with one or more of the other yachts—it was impossible to make an accurate assessment of the overall situation. Our moods varied from elation to depression as we got second and third hand reports of rivals' positions. Some of the details were several days old, others exaggerated, and yet more became inaccurate as they were transmitted between boats.

Sunday, September 23rd (Chay) DAY SIXTEEN
Day's run: 170 miles.

What a game! We spoke to *33 Export* this morning and he gave us Eric Tabarly's position. He was just south of Cape Verde Islands three days ago, which puts him at least 600 miles ahead of us. I could not understand how, but then Alec Honey suggested that he was copying the Blyth trick of trying to worry other competitors. If so, he has certainly succeeded in worrying me.

I have just heard Frank Page of *The Observer* giving the positions on the B.B.C. World Service so the information *33 Export* passed on must be wrong. Page puts *Pen Duick VI* first, *Burton Cutter* second, and us third. Based on the positions he gave we are only about 100 miles behind *Pen Duick,* which considering that we don't know how to sail is not bad. Tabarly is making seven miles a day more than us.

Each day we get better. I accept the fact that we will probably lose this leg but I shall be very angry if we lose the others.

We let the little bird go. It flew around the boat twice and then dived into the water. I felt sorry for it. It's probably long gone now.

Same Day (John).

It is very humid at the moment and everyone is looking forward to wash day; deodorant is a "must" for the next leg.

Alec stood down two men per watch last night so I was able to get a bit of sustained sleep. Alan Toone has just told us that we have got curry for supper tonight. In this heat. He must be a sadist.

Monday, September 24th (John) DAY SEVENTEEN
Day's run: 173 miles.

There's not a cloud in the sky and I think it is going to be really hot. There is very little wind—perhaps we are in the Doldrums already—but nevertheless morale is very high because we know Tabarly's position and he is not too far ahead.

We had a very good breakfast, cornflakes, fruit juice, fried egg and freshly baked bread. The sun is belting down and most of the lads are sunbathing on deck. I had a shower with sea water and it was quite refreshing. I did some laundry in the sea too but I will have to wait for some rain before I can rinse it out properly to get rid of the salt. The skipper will not allow fresh water for rinsing clothes—only rain water, and then you have got to collect it yourself.

The Port Watch saw a sword fish but it had gone by the time I got on deck. However I did see a school of about thirty dolphins and they were leaping 10 feet out of the water.

The Equator is now about 600 miles away. If these are the Doldrums then we should soon be running into the south-east Trades and then reaching most of the way to Cape Town. So far we have covered 2,728 miles.

We had spaghetti bolognese for dinner, which made a change.

Tuesday, September 25th (Chay) DAY EIGHTEEN
Day's run: 157 miles.

Another bird landed on deck and again we caught it and gave it a rest. It looked like a swallow but the trouble is that none of the crew know much about birds, well, not feathered ones anyway.

The winds are still very light. This is where we have to work like mad so that we get pulled through the water at a few knots. It is very hot and when you are off Watch you seek the shade. I heard *Burton Cutter* on the blower and he gave his position as 07° 20′ N but that can't be right. He would have to cover 200 miles a day for the last four days and that is seemingly impossible in this area.

Waiting for our turn on the radio we overheard a fascinating conversation. A happy chappy from the Merchant Navy was sending his fiancée a "Dear John" message. She pleaded with him and cried her eyes out. All the wedding arrangements had been made including taking a lease on a house. It got so bad that we had to switch off because the conversation became even more personal. I don't want the lads having bad dreams!

Same Day (John).

I am feeling a bit pensive today. I have been thinking what it is going to be like when I return to the Army. I've just about decided to come out but a lot will depend on Sandra. I can think of nothing worse than returning to muster parades and room inspections.

At the moment I am being plagued by a sweat rash, it would help if I could wash in fresh water every day. Most of us look like natives now, and we wear towels instead of shorts because it makes for better ventilation. The "Phantom Pincher"—he steals goodies—was at work during the night and the stock of biscuits had dwindled considerably.

Wednesday, September 26th (Chay) DAY NINETEEN
Day's run: 112 miles.

Nothing but squalls all day and night and we have to tack back and forth.

I spoke to Maureen and it really was terrific to hear her. It is her birthday today and I had arranged to have flowers sent to her. She was thrilled. All seems well at home and she sounded very cheerful, telling me that Samantha has settled down at school and that she loves the new flat down at Dartmouth.

Brian Daniels spoke to his wife Ruth.

Towards the end of the day it poured with rain. We collected lots of water and everyone took the opportunity to have a swill and wash their hair. It must have been quite odd seeing us prancing about nude in the pelting rain.

We sighted two very large whales basking in the sun but we disturbed them and they swam away. We had lightning all night, real Doldrums stuff.

Same Day (John).

There is very little wind, the sea is like glass, and to make matters worse that bloody spinnaker blew out again during the night. I will be glad when we get a new one in Cape Town. This blasted rash is giving me hell, especially at night. I am now washing it in disinfectant and using the good old Army "foot-and-body powder".

Last night Pete and Eddie nearly gave the skipper a coronary when they caught him at the orange juice. Perhaps he is the Phantom Pincher after all!

This must be the hottest day we have had so far and it is almost impossible to walk on the deck in bare feet. It is like an oven below deck.

So these are the Doldrums. I hope we are not stuck here for very long. We have now covered 3,000 miles and averaged 160 miles a day which is not bad considering all the light winds we have had.

The more I think about that light spinnaker and it blowing out again the wilder I feel. I think I will burn it on the foredeck. No, the skipper says repair it, so it's back to the drawing board. He thinks we will need it when we get to the Horse Latitudes, which is another area noted for its calms.

Thursday, September 27th (Chay) DAY TWENTY
No run recorded.

What a frustrating 24 hours. Struggling to get south, we were tacking back and forth all bloody day. The wind shifted from south-east to south-west with squalls, rain, and bad visibility. We have had to drop sails, put them up, reef, unreef—everybody is quite shattered.

Yet another bird landed on deck looking done in so we got him down below and shoved him in the aft compartment with some food and water. We decided to call him Terry Bond.

Bad news. Pete smashed the tip of his forefinger in a winch. He let out a scream like a stuck pig. However, the doc (Alan) gave him a pain-killing jab and dressed it. Pete seems quite comfortable now.

Friday, September 28th (John) DAY TWENTY-ONE
No recorded run.

It is Sandra's birthday today. I wish I was there to take her out. I will make up for it next year I hope. It is a good job you cannot wear out a photograph by looking at it otherwise hers would have disappeared long ago. It is going to crack me up if she finds someone else.

My sweat rash seems to be spreading and it is driving me up the bloody wall. I have tried just about everything to get rid of it and now I have dressings soaked in vinegar strapped to my crutch.

We should cross the Line [Equator] some time tonight or early in the morning. The skipper was unable to get a fix today so we do not know accurately how far we have travelled in the last day. However, the good news is that when he was speaking to the *Sunday Times* they told him that John Williams had managed to get space on a military aircraft for our spares.

Saturday, September 29th (Chay) DAY TWENTY-TWO
Day's run: 186 miles.

We are on the downhill run now! We crossed the Line at 11.25 G.M.T. at long. 47° 60′ west. We sailed across in great style at 10 knots. We celebrated with a wee dram of whisky and a digestive biscuit and then went back to work. This was my fifth crossing of the Equator. Brian was the only other to have crossed it at sea, this was his third time.

Same Day (John).

I changed the dressings on my crutch this morning and at last it looks as though the rash might be starting to clear up. Everyone seems quite concerned about the food situation. We had Alpen cereal and a bread roll for breakfast. We could do with more snacks during the day because we are all fed up with sucking barley sugars. Our feathered visitor, the one we named after Terry, finally died this morning. I don't think we expected him to survive but it was sad to see him go. It must have been all that curry we fed him. Anyway, morale has certainly risen now that we have crossed the Equator.

Sunday, September 30th (Chay) DAY TWENTY-THREE
Day's run: 229 miles.

Bad News. The running backstay has sunk into the deck with pressure. This means the foam has been compressed and that we have dents along the port and starboard of the deck in front of the winches.

We had an 'O' Group [a meeting of the whole crew at which orders are given and decisions made]. Before we sailed we were so concerned about weight that everything was cut down to a minimum including rations. Well, we have been eating more than we were entitled to and worse, I thought the leg to South Africa would take 40 days and it looks like at least 42. So we have to cut back on food. We will now be getting between 2,000 and 2,500 calories per day. It's a bit of a joke really and the chaps do not seem to mind too much. If anything, in some peculiar way it seems to add to the trip. One thing is certain, we will all lose weight on this leg. We have started to make out a goodies list for the next leg because weight will not be so important. The list is a couple of pages long already.

Same Day (John).

The sweat rash is showing signs of improvement, the vinegar appears to be doing the trick but it is certainly sore when I put it on.

The skipper told us that we will be able to take our wives and girl friends out for four or five days sailing when we get back. That's certainly something to look forward to. It cheered me up because I have been feeling a bit pensive again. I think I have just about decided to come out of the Army when I get back.

To pass the time when we are off watch we have organised a chess tournament. Yours truly was knocked out in the first round. We had a real treat, steak-and-kidney pie, for dinner tonight but I still felt hungry not long afterwards.

Monday, October 1st (Chay) DAY TWENTY-FOUR
Day's run: 188 miles.

I had two radio contacts today, one with Chris Waddington, the other with Jack Hayward. I gave Chris a couple of messages and he gave me the latest gen on the boating scene. But—surprise, surprise—he had not got a clue who was where in the race. He said the reports were so confusing and conflicting that he preferred to wait until we all got to Cape Town. I had a long chat with Jack and he sounded in great form, but then he always does. He sent his best wishes to the crew and said he hoped to get out to Sydney to see us. I felt a lot better after speaking to him. Somehow he gives me confidence. We're not dead yet! Attack!

Same Day (John).

I changed my dressings yet again and it seems to be finally clearing up. Alan is trying out an experiment with some rice pudding and Alpen cereal, and it looks as if it might turn out all right. Alan and the skipper are also working out the rations for the next leg. I hope this time we will have more goodies.

Tuesday, October 2nd (John) DAY TWENTY-FIVE
Day's run: 208 miles.

The wind has been quite light this morning and luckily it has come round so we are now flying a spinnaker. We heard some heartening news on the radio this morning. Apparently Tabarly crossed the Line after us so we are at worst level with him, *Adventure* is well over to the east of us, so it looks as though she is going to gamble on staying on the wind. She will have to come south sometime and must expect to lose some ground when she does. *CS e RB* seems to be going well but *33 Export* has dropped right back.

The wind this afternoon is almost non-existent and we are just ghosting along. We have kept up an average of 200 miles a day since we crossed the Equator but at this rate we will not be able to maintain it.

We actually had a bar of chocolate today—I don't think we will be able to put up with all this rich food. I managed to give the rash a good airing because we had time for a bit of sunbathing. We had the windseeker up this afternoon but it caught on one of the spreaders and is torn. A small patching job will soon put it right.

There was a fantastic red sunset this evening followed by an equally fantastic meal, curry and raspberries.

Wednesday, October 3rd (John) DAY TWENTY-SIX
Day's run: 168 miles.

I have been on deck most of the night and we have been plagued by light winds. We put the starcut spinnaker up but there seems to be something wrong with the cut of it.

We heard some positions of other yachts and it looks as though we are ahead but one can never tell. *Adventure* is coming our way and she has lost ground as a result. We are making between six and seven knots with the regular spinnaker and mizzen staysail. Len has been up the mast taking photographs and I think he found it rather lively up there because there is quite a sea running.

Soup yet again for lunch. We will all be about two stones lighter by the time we get to Cape Town. I know we are weight saving but this is ridiculous. Breakfast today consisted of cereal and a bread roll followed by coffee with saccharine. That stuff really is revolting. The skipper was in a strop today because of the light winds and the fact that our Watch managed to get the spinnaker wrapped around the backstay just for a change. I had to go up the shrouds and down the backstay to release it. Luckily there was no damage.

The skipper is teaching Alan and me how to work out sun sights. We will certainly have plenty of time to learn. The wind has picked up and we have the No. 2 Genoa up and a reefed main and we are doing between 9 and 10 knots.

The main topic of conversation among the lads is food. The skipper says it's a form of boredom. I say it's a form of hunger.

Thursday, October 4th (Chay) DAY TWENTY-SEVEN
Day's run: 180 miles.

We have light winds and then puffs up to Force 4. Where the hell are those "steady Trade winds" I keep reading about?

I heard one of the French yachts giving out handicap placings according to the French radio. They put *Pen Duick* first, *Great Britain* second, and *Adventure* fifth. Yesterday I heard a British yacht giving out handicap placings according to the B.B.C. and *Adventure* was first, *Pen Duick* sixth, and *Great Britain* seventh. I can imagine the Press getting so fed up with this sort of confused information that they will not bother to cover the race.

There was a near-calm all night. What a bloody game sailing is. Surely there is no more frustrating sport, because no matter what energy you put into it you rely on the wind. Out here it is worse because there is always a swell running. How we miss that light spinnaker!

Friday, October 5th (Chay) DAY TWENTY-EIGHT
Day's run: 137 miles.

Poor day's sail. Gales I don't mind but calms drive me up the wall.

I spoke to Tony Holden at the *Sunday Times* and he gave me some bad news and some good news. First the bad news—*Pen Duick VI* has been dismasted! This really is a blow to the race and he will be a big loss to the first leg. I hope he makes it to Cape Town for the start there; knowing Tarbarly he will if he possibly can. If there is any doubt, we should consider asking the Race Committee to postpone the restart until he can join us. At least no one was hurt in the dismasting. A mast coming down with sails, rigging, and so on could certainly smash a few limbs and even kill or knock someone overboard.

Now the good news. We knew that we were catching Tabarly up and because of his bad luck Tony says we are now leading the fleet both overall and on corrected time. I am amazed because I did not expect to do well on corrected time on this leg. Mind you, I do not put a lot of store on corrected time, it's elapsed time prizes that we are going for.

We sent Eric Tabarly a telegram of commiseration to Rio, where we understand he is putting in for repairs.

Same Day (John).

It's a shame about Tabarly and his mast but one cannot help feeling glad that it wasn't us. I think our skipper must be happy that we have got the strongest mast available. Even Tabarly remarked how strong it was when he looked over the boat back in U.K.

I suppose the biggest danger now is *Adventure*. She is doing very well for her size, but then the skipper always said that production boats would do better than "one-offs" on the first legs because they are proven and boats like ours are still finding their sea legs.

Back home John Williams was warming the Lonely Hearts by sending out his third Newsletter. He gave all the non-sailing snippets about such items as Pete's crushed finger (he omitted to mention John's sore crutch) and then went on to list the spares we had requested for Cape Town. It was a formidable collection, including 70 litres of paint and thinners; three sails (light spinnaker, starcut spinnaker, and light Genoa); engine hoses; five boom ends, a jockey pole and a jury rig; spare heavy weather sailing trousers; a winch; and Eddie Hope's reefer jacket and slacks which he had forgotten to put on board.

On the boat our morale was high. Although the lack of information meant that we could never be sure of our position in the race, we knew we were among the front runners. Even better, the wind suddenly started to come from the west and we began to zoom along at about 12 knots. On our twenty-ninth day at sea we covered 236 miles. We were working well as a crew. For relaxation we organised a chess tournament. To be precise there were two tournaments, one the Winners and one for the Losers. I won the Winners but then lost to Robbie of the Losers.

Sunday, October 7th (Chay) DAY THIRTY
Day's run: 196 miles.

> I have heard that *Adventure* is 300 miles nearer Cape Town than we are. They are really doing extraordinarily well, but I think they will have to slow up because there is a high pressure area right in their path.
>
> Great scoff today—curry with American rice. The chaps are starting to swop goodies among themselves. Brian gave Robbie two Horlicks tablets for one griddle cake. I think Robbie made a big mistake.
>
> We had an 'O' Group. I called it because someone was moaning the other night when he was called on deck to change a sail. The system is that if it is blowy and one Watch needs assistance I call everyone on deck. Someone (I do not know who) made a comment. At the 'O' Group I reminded them that our personal feelings do not count, only the aim of the exercise matters. I also warned them that I would send anyone back home who I considered did not fit into the

project as a result of the first leg. Finally I told the crew that, having sailed more than 5,000 miles non-stop, they could consider themselves experienced sailors.

Same Day (John).

It is getting noticeably colder although the temperature is still in the seventies. We had a real treat for NAAFI break today—five sardines and three Tuc biscuits. You can certainly see that some of us are losing weight, particularly the skipper, but then perhaps he can afford to lose more than the rest of us.

I ran out of cigarettes today but luckily Pete has given up smoking so now I'm using his supply.

Monday, October 8th (Chay) DAY THIRTY-ONE
Day's run: 155 miles.

Big personal disaster today. I said that a trip like this makes you physically weaker. Some of the chaps disagreed and Pete said he could do an average of 45 press-ups. He had a go but could only manage 15. Then John said he felt strong so I said (big mouth): "I bet you £1 you can't do 15 press-ups." John immediately did 15 so egged on by the others I agreed to double or quits against him doing 30. Of course he did them without any trouble so now I am £2 light.

All in all it has been a "get the money spent" day. I spoke with Maureen who sounded cheerful and told me she was getting on well with the refurnishing of the flat. She asked if she could go ahead and get oil-fired central heating installed. I said yes, but get a couple of quotes. Then she laughed and said she had already got four quotes and placed the order. One word from me and she does what she likes.

Adventure's progress continues to be good, but they must hit the high pressure sometime.

Spinnaker up for the first time in the Solent,
only two weeks before the start

Lifting *Great Britain II* to fit her keel (right of boat) and rudder

A pleasant day's sailing; some of the crew with HRH Princess Anne, Captain Mark Phillips, Jack and Susan Hayward

A few last-minute tips from Sir Alec Rose

The official presentations to HRH Princess Anne before the launch

The start of the race, Portsmouth, Septemb

ritain II leading, centre, *Pen Duick VI* astern

The author taking a sight

It may not look it, but she is doing 14 knots

Passing close to the Falkland Islands

A dangerous moment changing sail. The sail billows over the men. It was in similar circumstances that Paul Waterhouse was lost overboard from *Tauranga*

Off Rio's famous coastline

A squall brewing up off the eastern seaboard of South America

Same Day (John).

We have been at sea for a month now and everyone is really looking forward to getting across that finishing line at South Africa, if possible in first place. I know we were inexperienced and I know we did not expect to win this first leg, but I am sure it is what everyone secretly hopes.

The wind is not helping us. It is almost non-existent and the sails are banging back and forth. These calms get on everyone's nerves, particularly when we hear that *Adventure* is doing so well in an area noted for calms. The skipper spoke to Terry Bond today and he said we were getting good Press coverage in U.K. Personally, I would rather have a good wind.

John's hopes were realised. The wind was kind to us and again we were averaging more than 200 miles a day. However, such speed took its toll. The list of damage sustained in two days' sailing was:

Pulpit—broken free on one leg.
Spinnaker sheet—chafed through.
Two Handy Billies—pulled out and useless.
Lewmar block—split and useless.
Spinnaker pole—bent like a banana.
Two sails torn.

Such problems were naturally kept from our nearest and dearest back home, and John Williams chose to use his last "Lonely Hearts Newsletter" before setting out for South Africa to describe some of the plaques and presentations we had on board *Great Britain II*. He told them about the racing pennant, a blue Pegasus on a maroon background, presented to us by the Parachute Brigade Commander, Brigadier The O'Morchoe. Another gift with Brigade associations is the General (Boy) Browning Plaque. General Browning is known as the father of the Airborne Forces. He is now dead but his wife, the famous writer Daphne du Maurier, presented us with the plaque.

Winston Churchill has pride of place above the chart table. Underneath his photograph is a quote from one of his speeches. "At sea—resolution. Ashore—goodwill. In defeat—defiance. In victory—magnanimity." A source of inspiration, the picture was given to us by a friend, David Dyner.

By way of complete contrast we also display an extremely old framed verse given to us by Chris Waddington:

A Ship is called She
Because there is always a great deal of bustle about her.
Because she has a waist and stays,
Because she takes a lot of paint to keep her looking good,
Because it is not the initial expense that kills you—it's the upkeep,
Because she is all decked out,
Because it takes a good man to handle her right,
Because she shows her topside, hides her bottom, and when coming into port always heads for the buoys.

Thursday, October 11th (Chay) DAY THIRTY-FOUR
Day's run: 250 miles.

What a morning! I felt the yacht heeling over more than usual so I got out of bed. A squall had got up and the spinnaker pole was bent so I decided to drop the spinnaker and reach with the reaching sail. "All Hands," was called and the chaps came pouring out of their bunks, some in underpants, some nude. When everyone was assembled we were about to drop the pole when it broke and flew into the middle of the foredeck.

Bernie had gone forward to prepare for the spinnaker to come down and the foreguy or the pole hit him and knocked him over the bow. I cried out: "He's in the water."

The next ten minutes were quite fantastic. Brian threw over an automatic light which did not come on, and a lifebuoy. Len was on the helm and I shouted to him to call the course. I told Alan to watch the area but because it was still almost dark this was a near-impossibility. Robbie eased the spinnaker halyard and Mike organised pulling it in. I sent Brian down to start the engine and get a searchlight. Once the sail was in Len gave the time and course to Alec, who did a quick piece of mental arithmetic and gave Len a course to steer.

Everyone was stationed around the yacht in complete silence. We edged back against the wind using the engine. Eddie was sweeping the area with the searchlight.

Suddenly, faintly, we heard Bernie call out. I knew then that we would get him. He is not a strong swimmer but his suit with air trapped in it would help keep him afloat for a while.

We called and he answered, then Eddie picked him out in the searchlight. It was eerie and rather frightening to see him bobbing about in the blue of the water with the light shining on him. We threw him a line and he grabbed it, then five of the chaps lifted him out of the water.

"Are you all right Bernie?" I asked, thinking that maybe the boat had sailed over him and injured him in some way.

"The water's cold," was his only reply. He had been away from the yacht for seven minutes.

Same day (John).

After a drink of soup and a change of clothes Bernie was none the worse except for a few bruises. He was very, very lucky. The whole thing only took seven minutes but it seemed an age. I think every member of the crew realises that if you go overboard you have very little chance of being picked up.

We had good winds today and covered 250 miles, which is our record. It is excellent considering that we lost two hours while Bernie went for his swim.

Friday, October 12th (Chay) DAY THIRTY-FIVE
Day's run: 215 miles.

What lovely weather, nothing but squalls. It is Force 3 and then it rockets to Force 6. Reef in, reef out, No. 1 up, No. 1 down, No. 2 up, No. 2 down—what a bloody carry on. Progress is slow. We keep getting pushed on our side and that is useless for this boat, she must be sailed upright.

Same Day (John).

We had a reasonable breakfast this morning, cornflakes and a bread roll. However, the bread runs out tomorrow and I think we will all miss this little bit of luxury.

It is strange that *Adventure* has not been on the radio for the last few mornings. Normally if she is doing well she comes on the air prattling on about it. She is either going very well or very badly.

We are about 34° South now and should pick up the Westerlies any day. Brian and I have been working on the broken boom this afternoon, and we have inserted a sleeve and rivetted it into place. At least it should see us into Cape Town. We are now sailing hard on the wind with the No. 1 Genoa up and the No. 2 tied to the deck in case the wind gets up any more.

The next day The Man Who Makes Wind deserted us again and to make matters worse, I spoke with *Second Life* who were in a supposed high pressure zone and getting a Force 7 from the south-west. Then, as if that was not enough:

Sunday, October 14th (Chay) DAY THIRTY-SEVEN
Day's run: 159 miles.

For some time I have been suspicious that there is a Jonah on board, now I am sure of it. We have moved from a racing situation into a survival situation.

Alan was preparing tonight's food when he casually mentioned to Brian that there was something wrong with the water pump. Brian checked the mechanism and it seemed O.K. I suggested that we check the water tanks so we opened the top of the port side tank and looked inside. It was empty. We checked the starboard side which had been sealed off with an emergency amount of 30 gallons, and that too was empty.

Brian had checked both tanks about a week ago and reported that we had 100 gallons in the port tank and 30 gallons in the starboard one. I had told him to close the starboard tank and use the 100 gallons. We traced the fault to a loose fitting on the port tank which meant that while we were using the water it was draining away. A plastic fitting had been leaking on the starboard side and the whole 30 gallons had gone.

We had an emergency water supply but Alan worked out how much we would need to get us to Cape Town and it appears we are about 90 gallons short.

I called an 'O' Group to explain the situation and the alternatives to the crew. We are 1,060 miles from Cape Town, which is five days sailing at best and eight days at worst. We have emergency water and fluid (milk, juices) for 50 pints, which gives us a pint each for four days. We also have to expend tremendous energy sailing the boat at maximum speed and dropping spinnakers of up to 4,700 square feet.

We had a vote on the two alternatives—try to get through or ask for help and risk delay and possible disqualification from this leg. The vote was unanimous. We will only call for help when we cannot sail another inch. I wonder which way civilians would have voted?

Same Day (John).

At last I have managed to get my sailing trousers dry. They have been wet for ages and I had to rinse them out in rain water to get rid of the salt. I think wearing them damp aggravated my crutch rash. It has now completely cleared up and I am just left with a couple of bald patches where I had to give myself a trim.

Monday, October 15th (John) DAY THIRTY-EIGHT
Day's run: 172 miles.

During the night the wind was virtually non-existent and we were lucky to get 3 knots. Morale was a bit low this morning. We have had nothing to eat or drink now for 24 hours and we have only 50 pints of liquid on board including our survival packs and the juice in our canned foods. What we could do with now is a good rain shower and some decent wind. In fact the wind has just picked up a bit and we are doing about 8 knots which is encouraging but we are not getting a very good course. Breakfast was two digestive biscuits and two boiled sweets—I didn't really fancy scrambled eggs, crispy bacon, big banger sausages and a cup of Mother's tea anyway. We have got curry sauce without rice for dinner tonight, only because Alan prepared it before we knew we had run out of water.

In the last hour we covered only four miles. You just can't imagine how frustrating it is because every mile counts.

Last night Alan tried to boil sea water and condense it, but he did not seem to have much luck. It is going to be bloody hard if we come in second after all this.

Alan is going to try the pressure cooker again and so far he is managing to get a quarter-of-a-pint an hour from it. Lunch today was four sardines and two biscuits followed by two boiled sweets. Just the thing for growing lads. But the wine was a shade too warm for my liking.

Everybody is conserving as much energy as possible and we all get straight into out bunks as soon as we come off Watch. The skipper told us that lack of water can affect one's sex life and of course that cheered us up no end.

Bernie has been closely studying a book about the weather. Perhaps he has got a rain dance in mind. You certainly appreciate food and water when you haven't got any. Just think of all the water wasted in washing a car for instance, it seems almost criminal.

We have just had dinner, at least, I think we have. It was over so fast that it might have been my imagination. I have had a cup of hot blackcurrant juice and that was fantastic. It was our first drink for 24 hours. The lack of nourishment is starting to show, I feel quite tired. We had to get the No. 2 Genoa up on deck and it was a real effort. The skipper told us to wear our safety harnesses because our sense of balance will start to get worse.

Tuesday, October 16th (Chay) DAY THIRTY-NINE
Day's run: 207 miles.

We have some wind at last and everyone is quite cheerful. Early today I thought it was going to rain as a big black cloud approached, but no such luck, it passed over us without dispensing its load. Food today:

Breakfast —small amount of Alpen, $\frac{1}{3}$ cup milk.
NAAFI break — one shortbread biscuit, $\frac{1}{8}$ pint water.
Lunch — 6 sardines, 2 Tuc biscuits.
NAAFI break — $\frac{1}{8}$ pint milk, 2 barley sugars.
Dinner — $\frac{1}{3}$ of a delicious Fray Bentos steak pie,
2 small spoonfuls of peas.
Late tonight — $\frac{1}{8}$ pint water, 2 sweets.

The wind has dropped again tonight so we are

wallowing about. Morale is getting low and I pray all the time for rain and wind.

Wednesday, October 17th (John) DAY FORTY
Day's run: 101 miles.

We have been becalmed all night. We had done 53 miles by 08.00. We have just put up the spinnaker and we are making 5 knots, if it was not so serious it would be laughable. We only have two on Watch at a time now and the most simple jobs seem to take a great deal of effort. The skipper said that once we get in we will look back on this and wonder what all the fuss was about. Mike's reply was too disgusting even for my log book.

Same Day (Chay).

We should have arrived in Cape Town today but because of these calms we are still 500 miles away. Still, that's sailing!

We seem to have solved the water situation thank God. Cookie (Alan Toone) has fixed a Calor gas tube to the top of the pressure cooker. This leads into a bowl of salt water used for cooling and then the drinking water drips into a pot. We are getting just under two pints an hour and so far we have made 12 pints. It should work until we run out of gas and we have got quite a lot of that. I would like to place on record our grateful thanks to Tower Brand household products. You make great pressure cookers!

The sad thing is that most of our remaining food is dehydrated and I reckon we are now down to about 800 calories a day.

Thursday, October 18th (Chay) DAY FORTY-ONE
Day's run: 63 miles.

Another day of calms. Boy, did I draw a lousy

course when I chose this one! Still, chin up. Remember we're British.

The S.A. Maritime Shackleton flew over us today. We spoke over the radio and I'm sorry to say its radio operator had no sense of humour.

He said: What is your position?

I said: Why, are you lost?

He replied: Negative.

So I forgot the funnies and gave him my position.

We are still struggling on with the distilling plant and it is going great guns. We could not have picked anyone better for the galley. Alan is doing a terrific job.

One or two of the crew are getting edgy again. I have resigned myself to the fact that we are going to lose this leg and I think the chaps know it too. I am trying to make the most of the situation by testing the men. I have tried to promote a couple of arguments but although some of them start to bite they soon drop it. This proves that all those lectures and courses in Scotland are paying dividends because we are at our lowest ebb now—hungry, tired, physically weak, frustrated by the calms, and we face the defeat of our ambition to come into Cape Town first.

Our food today was—

Breakfast: cornflakes and $\frac{1}{8}$ pt. milk and $\frac{2}{3}$ cup of coffee.

Lunch: 6 sardines (I am fed up with bloody sardines) and two biscuits.

Afternoon break: $\frac{1}{3}$ cup coffee and two boiled sweets.

Dinner: Half-plate of dehydrated stew and $\frac{2}{3}$ cup coffee.

Same Day (John).

I started to wash down the decks this morning and gave Eric a rude awakening because he was asleep in his bunk and I had not noticed that one of the skylights was open. For the last few days we have had some big black birds for company, they just swoop down over the waves around the boat. I hope they are only waiting for fish.

The wind is coming in light puffs and Alec thought it was time to fly the spinnaker. He might just as well have tried to fly a double decker bus. We spoke to John Williams on the radio link and he told us that *Burton Cutter* is 350 miles from Cape Town so they are obviously well in the lead. It is very depressing when one considers that we were leading at one stage by 500 miles.

Len has been getting his kit ready for Cape Town by pressing his best trousers under the saloon seat. I have been getting mine ready as well. I have taken the waist in about three inches.

Friday, October 19th (Chay) DAY FORTY-TWO
Day's run: 145 miles.

At long last the wind has arrived and we are romping along. We can only pray that it holds out for the next 48 hours. I would even welcome a gale!

We sent three telegrams home. One was from Eric to his wife Peggy for their fifth wedding anniversary. He has only spent two anniversaries with her, but that is one of the penalties of being in the Paras. Another was a "good luck" message to Mike's little girl who is going to have an operation on Monday. The last was to my friend Chick Gough in Cape Town because I have lost his telephone number.

As far as we know no boat has arrived in Cape Town yet but it seems that *Burton Cutter* will be first there. Good old Les. It really could not happen to a nicer guy!

Same Day (John).

Everyone is feeling a lot weaker, which is hardly

surprising when you remember that we have been on a restricted diet for about twenty days now. Lunch today was half a bowl of soup and two oatcakes. I don't know how Robbie is surviving because he cannot stand dehydrated meals so he always has a bowl of cornflakes instead. We call him "The Cornflakes Kid".

The skipper has just taken a sight and we have 387 miles to go.

Saturday, October 20th (John) DAY FORTY-THREE
Day's run: 200 miles.

We had good winds throughout the night and finished with a reef in the mainsail and the No. 3 Genoa up. We had covered 145 miles by 06.00. Soon we had to change to the No. 2 Genny and take the reef out of the main because the wind started to drop again. It is becoming a great effort to change sails but we are spurred on by the thought that Cape Town is only 24 hours away and when we get there we can eat and eat and rest.

We should soon be sighting some ships, which will keep us alert at night. Now we have put the No. 1 Genoa up because the wind has dropped further and the skipper says we may have to tack which will be a bit of a drag because it means lost miles.

The skipper tried to get through to Cape Town Radio this morning. Reception was very bad and when eventually he did make contact it was only to hear that *Burton Cutter* had just crossed the line. It was a big, big disappointment. If we had only had decent weather we would have been in days ago. Never mind. We may have lost the battle but not the war. Anything can happen on the next three legs.

We have started to clean up ourselves and the boat, and both of us need it. Alan gave us our last cooked meal on board for a while—would you believe curry and raspberries?

Sunday, October 21st (John) DAY FORTY-FOUR

We had a good blow of 20 to 25 knots during the night. When I came on watch it was gusting 30 knots and we had to change down to the No. 3 to get closer to the wind. We are holding a good speed of 10 knots.

The skipper has just taken a sight and gives our E.T.A. as 17.00 hours. We are celebrating by finishing the rest of the food, dehydrated apple and rich cake. The only thing left edible on board is curry powder, lots and lots of it.

Land was sighted at 12.05 hours. *Adventure* crossed the line just before us and we sailed over at 16.53 hours precisely. We had a lot of trouble actually crossing the line because the winds were very flukey. One minute we had two reefs in the main, the next we had the windseeker up.

We had to get a tow from a police launch when we got into the actual harbour because our drive failed. We tied up alongside an Iranian destroyer.

As we stepped ashore the wind was blowing 40 knots.

PART THREE

Cape Town—Sydney

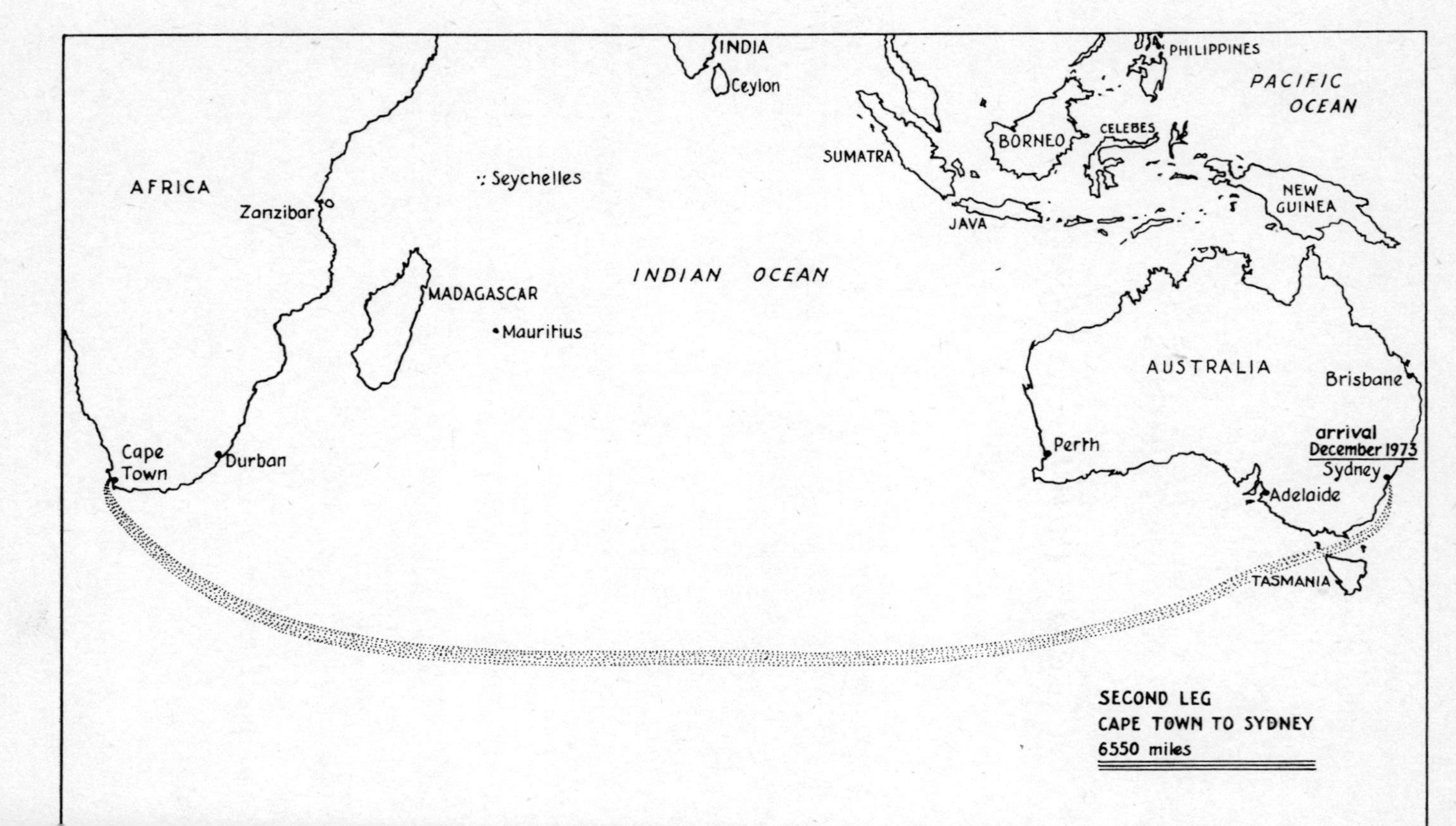
INDIA
Ceylon
PHILIPPINES
PACIFIC OCEAN
AFRICA
Zanzibar
Seychelles
SUMATRA
BORNEO
CELEBES
NEW GUINEA
JAVA
INDIAN OCEAN
MADAGASCAR
Mauritius
AUSTRALIA
Brisbane
Perth
arrival December 1973
Sydney
Adelaide
TASMANIA
Cape Town
Durban
SECOND LEG
CAPE TOWN TO SYDNEY
6550 miles

7

Cape Town is Table Mountain. At least, that is the impression we got as we sailed into the harbour because it dominates the entire scene. It was a relatively clear day and there was a north-easterly wind blowing to form clouds on top of the mountain. The wind whisked the clouds around and they seemingly spilled from its flat top like a huge and erupting volcano. The effect was breathtaking because the mountain had both majesty and movement, and it was some time before we took in the rest of the impressive panorama, the Twelve Apostle mountains and the skyscraper vista that is Cape Town.

There were the usual formalities when we had tied up. Dozens of officials came on board, we toasted our arrival in the traditional champagne, and received the congratulations on our voyage. It was only when I looked across at *Burton Cutter* and *Adventure* that I felt the first pangs of annoyance and contrition. We had arrived third and no amount of talk could alter that.

My depression was staved off by the arrival of the man I regard as my best friend, Chick Gough. He is a fellow Scot and a professional footballer playing for the Johannesburg club Highlands Park. His team had been playing Cape Town in a league fixture and he had stayed on for a couple of days to have a get-together. While the crew went for a beer and a yarn at the yacht club I went with Chick to his hotel. I was looking forward to my first bath in more than six weeks but, as experience had taught me, it was all something of an anti-climax. While you are at sea you dream about a bath and relish the thought but when it actually happens it is just another bath, all very disappointing.

After a brisk towelling I dressed in my reefer and flannels and rejoined the crew at the yacht club. We had a superb dinner, a huge blow-out of soup and steak and chips and sticky sweet and cheese and beer and wine and coffee. This certainly was not an anti-climax, it lived up to our anticipations and afterwards everyone felt tired, bloated, and happy.

The crew slept on board *Great Britain II* and I went with Chick back to his room. Alec told me next day that the men just flaked out as soon as they got back on board because it had been such an exhausting day. I envied them because I was feeling decidedly morning-after-the-night-beforeish. Chick and I had taken a bottle of Scotch to his room and it was the wee small hours when we finally crawled to our beds.

After reminiscing on old times and listening to the style of Chick's life in South Africa, I began to tell him about the trip. It was then, the first time that I had been able to look at the journey in retrospect, that real depression set in. We had come third. We were getting better but would we be able to pull it out of the bag? The more I thought about it the more worried I became. Chick offered words of encouragement, emphasising the points in our favour and minimising our shortcomings. He is however a realist and must have realised that the cards were stacked against us.

Despite the Scotch I hardly slept that night. Worry is not exactly foreign to my nature but rarely does it affect me to any extent. This time though I was in a deep depression and it was as much as I could do to keep it from the crew. I talked things over with Major Calier, Project Manager for the Army's *British Soldier* team, but he could do little more than reaffirm his faith in our ability. After three more sleepless nights I began to feel really ill and went along to Robin Leach, the doctor on *Second Life*, for a thorough examination. He confirmed that there was nothing physically wrong with me and gave me some strong sleeping pills to counteract my insomnia.

The pills worked and with sleep my confidence began to return. However, I rarely left the boat during the day and where it was not too impolite to do so I excused myself from the tour of parties and dinners that were such a pleasant feature of our stay in Cape Town. There was so much to do on the boat as far as repairs and re-organisation were concerned that I wanted to make every moment in port count.

Cape Town has a reputation for hospitality and it was daily demonstrated to us. Complete strangers would come to the boat with bunches of flowers, presents, and drinks. We were invited out literally every night. We were given the free use of a car. The generosity was seemingly endless and I doubt whether it could be matched at any port in the world.

Our crew were particularly lucky to meet Captain Philip Nankin who is head of Cape Town's Merchant Navy Academy. He offered all of us accommodation at the Academy and he and his wife were perfect hosts.

The friendliness of the South Africans is infectious and transmitted itself to the crews. In Portsmouth before we left there had been a cautious acknowledgment of the existence of the other yachts but no real mateyness. Now, however, we had shared an experience and survived, we were going to face more dangers and exhilarations and there was a mutual respect and friendship between the competitors. We invited each other to parties on board and we explored the delights of Cape Town together. Only one thing happened to mar our South African stay. Captain Brian Daniels, our engineer, had to return to Britain for personal reasons, and our crew was down to eleven.

All too soon Wednesday November 7th was upon us and we lined up to face the Southern Ocean. Tabarly had rejoined the race so once again I considered him the man to beat. We got off to a great start because we scored a tactical point over Eric and he was not too happy about it. The winds were light and I, in common with a number of others including *Burton Cutter, Pen Duick,* and *Kriter,* decided that the best thing would be to cross the line at a point farthest away from the gun. About a minute before the gun went off *Kriter* was just ahead of *Pen Duick* and I was third. Then *Kriter* luffed up *Pen Duick,* which meant that he was trying to put Eric the wrong side of the buoy, making him come round again. Eric saw the strategy and tried to come behind *Kriter* and slip in astern of her. I saw what Eric planned, shot across, and blocked his entrance. Eric had three choices, to hit us, hit *Kriter*, or to go the wrong side of the buoy. Obviously he went round the buoy, then had to turn round and go back again. He was livid. I have a clear mental picture of him jumping up and down and shouting in anger at his crew. I also saw Jack Grout, skipper of *Kriter,* doubled up with laughter.

Nobody scores over Eric for long and soon he had sliced his way through the fleet to take the lead.

Thursday, November 8th (Chay) DAY TWO
Day's run: 147 miles.

> During the night there was a terrific bang and automatically the Watch Officer, Mike, called "All Hands". At first, because of the darkness, it was difficult to see what had happened. Then we saw it—a sail had been tied down ready to change. The change had not been needed so foolishly we had left the sail there. The water had plucked at it until eventually the sheer weight pulled two stanchion bases out and broke the stanchions. The sail was torn and it took us about 20 minutes to get it below. What a good start to the leg!

All day we have had a yacht looming behind us but she is too far off to be identified with any certainty. It is a ketch with a dark hull so it could be *Kriter* or *Pen Duick*.

There is a fine atmosphere now among the competitors and we have long yarns with the other yachts. Eric Pascoli is a great joker, he gives everyone a different position because he says his yacht is moving so fast it keeps changing.

Friday, November 9th (Chay) DAY THREE
Day's run: 220 miles.

I was rudely awakened at 05.00 to be told that the regular spinnaker had blown. Boy, what a mess! A 40 knot squall had hit us without warning and the sail had blown right out. It took us over an hour to sort things out but the sail is in shreds and we have no chance of repairing it. This is where we lose the miles. The wind has been all over the place in varying strengths. We change from light sails to regular spinnaker then starcut and then continually to No. 3 and reefed main.

Pete spoke to his new girlfriend in Cape Town. I suggested he propose to her because it would make a nice piece for the *Sunday Times* weekly story, but he did not seem too keen.

Saturday, November 10th (Chay) DAY FOUR
Day's run: 225 miles.

The wind has been blowing at near gale force since yesterday. We are hard on the wind and slamming into the seas. Alan and Pete have been sick. The constant smashing has brought inevitable damage, with two wash hand basins pulled away from the bulkhead and one of the fuse boxes smashed.

Sunday, November 11th (Chay) DAY FIVE
No run recorded.

Sad news. We heard on the radio that *Burton Cutter* is having to retire. I called up Les Williams and he confirmed it. The plates in the bow of *Burton Cutter* were opening up and she was leaking badly. I am genuinely sorry because it is always sad to lose competitors, especially the good guys like Les. We will miss him and his crew in the race and in the ports.

More bad news. Eddie Hope has fractured his right forearm in a fall. We called up *Second Life* and Dr Leach told Alan how to set the arm for the next thirty days.

Same Day (John).

It is still blowing like hell, 40 knots at times, and we have the No. 4 Genoa up but still no main, even so we are doing between 9 and 11 knots. Safety harnesses are the order of the day and you certainly need them on this deck. I was working on the lee side when a wave hit me and washed me around the winch. I was bloody glad I had my harness on.

The spray coming over the deck is making it difficult for the helmsman to see the compass. Mike had the good idea of using divers' masks and it is quite a funny sight to see a man at the helm with a diver's mask on. With the amount of water coming over we could do with flippers as well. Everyone and everything is soaked, even our sleeping bags.

Monday, November 12th (Chay) DAY SIX
No run recorded.

We spoke to Robert Leach again about Eddie's arm because it is still giving him pain. Tomorrow we are going to put it in a Fibreglass splint because we have lost the plaster of paris.

The meals are a bit different on this leg. Tonight we

had gammon steak (compliments to Cape Town Rotary Club), peas, boiled potatoes, and tomatoes. We almost had Mike's boiled head as well because he complained to Cookie that there were not any pineapple rings.

We found a case of avocado pears which Alan had forgotten about. Sadly, most of them were bad, which is a crying shame when you consider the price of them in U.K. and the fact that I like avocados. Alan now tells me that he can't find the cheese but no doubt we will find it—or rather smell it—in a few days.

We are no longer a "dry ship", although the Press at home made great play on the fact that I had banned all alcohol from *Great Britain II*. I have decided that I know the men well enough now so each day we have a Happy Hour, when we relax and maybe take a wee dram—just one, mind.

For the next few days we had varying winds and we pushed *Great Britain II* to her limit. Eddie's arm was in a bad way and Bernie almost burned him to death when he put the glass fibre on, but nevertheless the morale of the crew was high. Every morning at 11.00 G.M.T. we would chat via the radio to other competitors and it was obvious that we were doing very well indeed. One of our most memorable days was Princess Anne's wedding to Captain Mark Phillips. We sent them a telegram to Buckingham Palace. It read:

CONGRATULATIONS AND SINCERE GOOD WISHES. PLEASE CANCEL HONEYMOON—MARK NEEDED AS HELMSMAN. FROM CREW *GREAT BRITAIN II*. We heard that they were honeymooning in the Royal Yacht *Britannia* and thought of trying to arrange a rendezvous off Cape Horn.

One of the fascinating topics of conversation among the crew was Pete's new romance with a young lady called Pam in Cape Town. Communications with South Africa were becoming more difficult as we moved further away and if he missed his regular ship-to-shore call he sulked all day. However, she did manage to get through on his birthday and because of the poor reception I had to stay on the radio with him and tune it in when it faded. It was most embarrassing—what it is to be young and in love!

Friday, November 16th (Chay) DAY TEN
Day's run: 253 miles.

I spoke to the *Sunday Times* and told them about Eddie's arm. Then I had a great call to Maureen. She sounded cheerful and I know it is genuine because if there is any trouble she cannot hide it from her voice. The best news of all is that she is bringing Samantha out to Sydney with her. Not so good news is that she has smashed her car and done £250 worth of damage. I laughed—what else could I do?—after all she has had it all of two months. Anyway, she was not hurt in the crash and that is the main thing.

Another spinnaker has blown. It looked pretty trailing in the water behind. It looked pretty expensive too, and I am not going to enjoy asking Jack Hayward if I can order two more storm and one regular spinnakers.

Same Day (John).

I seem to do nothing but repair sails. The weather is getting cold now and a few of the lads are already wearing their thermal suits. I imagine it is going to get colder because the skipper has started to use a hot water bottle.

We had our second best run today. *Adventure* is 460 miles behind, and we heard on the radio that we are leading Tabarly. We are maintaining a speed of between 10 and 11 knots.

Saturday, November 17th (Chay) DAY ELEVEN
Day's run: 275 miles.

Cookie had a sulky face today and because it was most unusual for him I asked him what was the matter. "Nothing," he replied. "It's just that everyone else seems to get sulky sometimes so I thought it might as well be my turn." Anyway, I have decided we take him too much for granted. I have had a word with Alec and Mike and from now on the Watches will help him wash up the coffee cups. However, there will be no other interference because the galley is his domain.

We have now got six helmsmen, Eric, Len, Mike, Robbie, Bernie and me. Eric and Bernie had never been on a boat before, yet they are helming a 77 foot monster doing 15 knots.

The critics can knock me but they sure as hell can't knock my crew. We have two Watches of four on the boat plus a skipper and a cook (one man has a broken arm and so cannot be counted). There should be 16 or even 18 men on board but my theory about paratroopers is proving right. They will put up with more and work harder without complaint than any other bunch of men. We are taking on the world's best yachtsman in Eric Tabarly, he has got a boat as fast if not faster than ours, and he is worried. So he should be. The honeymoon's over and we are ready. Attack!

Eddie is having difficulty sleeping with the pain from his arm. We feel so helpless because there is nothing we can do except give him a pain-killing pill when it gets too much. We will have to be careful not to get him hooked. He helps by doing maintenance down below but the danger is that the slightest jar sends a screaming pain up his arm.

I sent our exact position—44°S 60°E—to Race Control. *Pen Duick* came up on the radio trying to contact us but I refused to answer. The Race Committee requested that boats should give their positions, weather and barometer readings to all other yachts each day at 11.00 G.M.T. Everyone has complied with the request except *Pen Duick*. Now the yachts are beginning to level out and he is keen to know what latitude we intend to stay at, so that he can decide whether to go further south. Well, we are not in the race to suit Eric's convenience; as they say in the Paras, "He can leg it."

Bernie was doing the hourly check at 01.45 hours when he noticed that the outhaul on the spinnaker was chafing through. He called me from my bed and within twelve minutes we had changed outhauls. That may seem quite simple to the uninitiated but the change meant:

1. Getting a spare sheet and shackle from below.
2. The pole forward controlled by four men—the outhaul, guy, foreguy, and topping lift.
3. Foredeck man reefing stout line around forestay.
4. Making fast to tack of spinnaker with line.
5. Weight taking off overhaul and taken up with forestay line.
6. New outhaul reefed.
7. Outhaul made fast and weight taken.
8. Line taken off.
9. Pole aft and up.
10. All the time the spinnaker is being controlled by two men on the coffee grinders.

Same Day (John).

About a dozen dolphins have been with us this morning. They are fascinating to watch, they swim alongside us and then dive under the bows and reappear on the other side.

It is still uncomfortably cold and damp and the sky is overcast so I doubt whether the skipper will be able to take a sun sight. It is supposed to be wash and shave day today but it is so cold and miserable that I guess only the very brave will take advantage of it.

Sunday, November 18th (Chay) DAY TWELVE
Day's run: 282 miles.

High drama today. At 07.15 hours during Alec's Watch I decided we would put a second reef in the mainsail while the spinnaker was still up. I took the helm while the Watch put the reef in. The danger comes when you have to sheet the mainsail in to get the topping lift on and sufficiently inboard to get the reef in. Wind is pushed on to the main and pressures the bow into the wind. If a problem occurs then the normal thing is to let the main sheet fly and this helps to control the boat. Unfortunately for us, she started to come up into the wind and we could not let the main go because Eric was on the end and it would have been too dangerous. So the worst happened. We broached at 15 knots. The boat crashed on to its side to an angle of approximately 70°. The mainsail flapped like hell, I still had full lock on the helm, and I shouted to everyone to hang on. The spinnaker boom broke and luckily its end jaws opened and the spinnaker flew out. The pole crashed on to the deck and I cried: "All Hands!" There we were, beam on and the spinnaker flying out at right angles to us. I put one man on the outhaul and another on the halyard and let the spinnaker drop into the water. With the main down and dragging the spinnaker the yacht was still doing two knots. Eventually we pulled the sail inboard and with two reefs and a No. 3 we got under way again.

Same Day (John).

The barometer is still dropping and it looks as though this blow is going to continue for some time. The skipper has just taken a sight and we have had our best day's run, more than 280 miles. It means that we have done more than 1,000 miles in four days. Not bad for amateurs. The chart on the saloon wall is having great chunks carved out of it and we will soon be halfway.

Monday, November 19th (Chay) DAY THIRTEEN
Day's run: 218 miles.

It all happens in the Southern Ocean. Already one spinnaker and boom lost and now would you believe the mizzen mast! How it occurred is still a bit of a mystery. I told Alec to get the mizzen spinnaker up and we had the No. 3 boomed out and one reef in the mainsail. As the chaps got the sail ready I went below. Suddenly there was a terrific bang and I shot back on deck certain that the boom had gone again. Instead I saw the mizzen mast down and jammed on the mainsail. How it did not go through the sail I will never know; it reflects great credit on Ratsey's sails. My first reaction was to rename the whole of the Watch with unprintable words. Instead I must confess I laughed. An unfortunate idiosyncracy of mine is that the worse the situation, the funnier I find it. It is probably an escape valve for emotions but I believe it is better than displaying anger or fear, although one has to be careful otherwise those watching would think I had become demented and reached the giggly stage.

The immediate requirement was to get the mizzen down from its precarious perch. Len went aloft in the Bosun's Chair to tie a line around the mast head in order to take the weight. Another line was attached from the masthead to the broken after part of the mizzen and in this way we could take the weight and lower the mast on to the deck. When it was down we tried in vain to dismantle it; we ended up by lashing it to the deck. All the rigging had to be stripped off and stowed. With no mizzen we will lose some balance and speed. This is bad news indeed.

Via the radio grapevine we have just heard some very sad news. A crew member on *Tauranga* has been lost overboard; he was hit by a spinnaker boom. I have prayed for the man's family and for Eric Pascoli, the skipper of *Tauranga*. Knowing Eric, he will take it very badly, fortunately his wife is on board so she will help him get over it.

When I heard about the man overboard, my mind flashed to that time on the first leg when Bernie was lost for seven minutes. Losing a man is the skipper's nightmare. One can always replace masts, sails, equipment, but for a man to be lost is a dreadful finality. I take comfort from the thought that if he had to go, if his number was up, then it is better to go through the front door struggling and fighting for his very existence. Surely it is better than being mangled in some miserable car crash on land, where the happening is so commonplace that people are almost blasé about it.

Tuesday, November 20th (John) DAY FOURTEEN
Day's run: 230 miles.

We are sustaining so much damage in these seas that it is a wonder there is a bloody boat left. Last night at around 23.00 hours we tried to hoist the spinnaker but it got fouled up in the rigging before it had reached the masthead. The rolling of the boat did not help and so we decided to drop the sail. It fell in front of the yacht and we sailed right over it. When we got it on board it was ripped for about two-thirds of its length. We then tried to put up the storm spinnaker and—would you believe?—exactly the same thing happened again. Luckily there was very little damage this time. At about 05.30 we managed to get a spinnaker up.

It is not inexperience that is causing this damage. The physical conditions are extreme and every man and piece of equipment is being tested. Men are becoming exhausted because in extreme conditions we could do with more hands.

When we had the spinnaker up we were really screaming along. The wind and the waves built up and it was a hairy experience surfing off the top of the waves. The wind has increased to 20 knots apparent 30/35 knots true and the pole started to flex under the strain. Suddenly we were slewed round by a wave and broached. The spinnaker pole snapped and the pole flew up leeward. We had one hell of a job getting it in.

The Watch system was abandoned and we set about repairing the damage to the sails and poles. Everyone worked like mad and by 18.00 hours we were finished.

We have heard that Tabarly is slightly behind us and this is good to know. We are now about 300 miles south of Amsterdam Island and halfway to Sydney. I will be glad when we get there. Before we left the experts said that the Roaring Forties would test the yacht and its crew. They were absolutely right. At the moment our deck looks like a scrap metal yard.

Eddie, with his one good hand, is proving a master chef. Tonight he prepared stewed steak, fish pie, and cake.

Wednesday, November 21st (Chay) DAY FIFTEEN
Day's run: 215 miles.

I sent a telegram to Maureen. It read: PUSHING HARD. MIZZEN MAST GONE. BOTH SPINNAKER POLES BROKEN ALSO SPINNAKERS. BOND TO INVESTIGATE INSURANCE. EXPENSIVE HOBBY. REPLY MELBOURNE. LOVE YOU. CHAY. I sent it via *Adventure* and coincidentally they had a message from Buckingham Palace for us. TO SKIPPER AND CREW GREAT BRITAIN II. WE WERE DELIGHTED TO RECEIVE YOUR MESSAGE. THANK YOU

VERY MUCH ANNE. You can imagine how that has cheered us up. The chaps think Princess Anne and Mark Phillips are the greatest thing since sliced bread.

The one-armed Eddie has gone berserk, making us a fantastic raspberry pie decorated with orange. He got congratulations from everyone except Alec who is not too happy with life today. He was sound asleep when a big wave broke over the boat, the aft hatch was open, and Alec was soaked. He blamed Eric who was on the helm at the time.

Late tonight I decided to match Eddie's culinary achievements by cooking crêpes suzette for everyone. It is not generally known that I am a crêpes suzette king. I was liberal with the brandy and on the first occasion that I lit one Pete, who was asleep, shot out of his bunk and on to deck because he thought the boat was on fire. I used three-quarters of a bottle of brandy and as a result the crêpes tasted beautiful. I had two myself and felt quite giddy.

Now we were really moving and every day our runs were nearer 250 miles than 200. The spirit among the crew was tremendous. Everyone was efficient at their specialist jobs and able to assist others competently when help was needed. The fellowship of the Parachute Regiment was permanently evident.

Our better halves were being comforted back in England via the John Williams sixth "Lonely Hearts Newsletter." He started by explaining some of the troubles we had encountered and then went on:

The loss of the mizzen will slow the yacht down but she will still be able to sail to Sydney quite safely. The long radio aerial was attached to the mizzen mast so now they are working the radio on a 14 foot whip aerial. This means instead of having a contact range of thousands of miles they are reduced to about 800 miles and any messages have to be relayed via another yacht.

We have ordered another mast from the makers, Sparlight, and they are working round the clock to make it in time to reach *Great Britain II* in Sydney.

Enclosed with this letter are two photographs. One was taken from a South African Air Force plane and the other shows *Great Britain II* crossing the start at Cape Town with Table Mountain in the background. Jack Hayward has ordered a special Christmas card showing *Great Britain II* under sail and we will be dispatching you a dozen each to send to relatives and friends.

Sailing at this constantly high speed was taxing to both mind and body and occasionally there had to be lapses. Thus my log records:

Saturday, November 24th (Chay) DAY EIGHTEEN
Day's run: 271 miles.

Robbie got aggro with Alec today. Robbie was alone at the helm and the Starboard Duty Watch was below dressed and ready to come on deck at a moment's notice. The signal for assistance is a shrill whistle and at the end of his turn at the helm Robbie whistled. He wanted his relief to take over. He whistled again, nothing. Eventually he started to shout at the top of his voice and this woke me and half of the Off Watch as well as those on duty. Every man on the Starboard Watch had fallen asleep and Robbie was angry. He gave the Watch Officer, Alec, a very graphic run down on what he consideted a Watch Officer's duties to be.

Alec agreed and apologised and the whole incident was over in a couple of minutes. The danger was of course that something could have been wrong when Robbie whistled so after things had cooled down I had a word with both Watches. It will not happen again and it was a lesson worth learning.

Same Day (John).

We have had the spinnaker up all night so we should have a good day's run. We are now about 1,000 miles south west of Perth and should be in the Bass Strait in about a week.

Pete and I finally finished the repair job on the regular spinnaker so now I suppose we will have to start on the No. 2 Genoa. It will be quite a long task but at least it will be easier than working on the fine material of the spinnaker.

We heard on the radio that *Sayula* has not been reporting her position to Race Control and could possibly be liable to a penalty. Nothing has been heard of *Copernicus* or *Peter von Danzig* for a couple of days but nobody is too woried because communications in this part of the world are difficult. The Met. Check this afternoon indicated that we will probably be getting another gale within the next few days because there is a cold front approaching. There is very little sea running now which makes life below much more comfortable.

Monday, November 26th (Chay) DAY TWENTY
Day's run: 298 miles.

The best day's run so far. It could have been over the 300 mile barrier if I had kept the No. 3 up but it was getting a bit hairy so I dropped to the No. 4. I had a taste of personal danger today. I was standing in the cockpit watching Bernie helm when a wave broke over the stern and lifted me bodily out of the cockpit. I managed to grab hold of the mizzen stump and hang on, Bernie was forced to let go of the wheel and was thrown on his side but luckily he had his safety harness on. Such things happen without warning and are over in a couple of seconds but they serve as reminders of the dangers of the sea.

The weld on the pulpit has gone again so we have had to put ties near the foot of the sail, which does not help the set of the sails but helps the pulpit.

In contrast to the first leg we are eating well and have plenty of goodies. Today sweeties for the next ten days were issued so we each have a stock of Crunchies, Picnic bars and Curly Wurlys—no wonder we are all putting on weight. The only item we are short of is gas and we are down to our last bottle. The oddity is that we had plenty of gas on the first leg but we did not carry any more bottles. Eric, our plumber, reckons it is because the present gas is not such good quality as that which we had on the first leg and therefore it takes longer to heat the food. I can't make up my mind whether he is kidding me or not.

The compass is surging like mad in this Southern Hemisphere. Ideally one should have a compass with its needle counterpoised for the hemisphere's magnetic dip but then this would have meant more expense. We will put up with the one we have.

We have just realised that our run, 298 miles, is only eight miles off the official record for a conventional yacht. Not bad for amateurs, and amateurs without a mizzen at that!

Tuesday, November 27th (John) DAY TWENTY-ONE
Day's run: 248 miles.

To get the most out of the yacht in these very flukey winds we are constantly changing sails. We have to adapt to conditions quicker than the other boats if we are to beat them home. We managed to get the spinnaker up this morning but then the wind died

The broken mizzen mast: above, it has twisted and gone forward, hitting the mainsail. Bernie is aloft helping to lower it. Below, sorting out the broken mast on deck

Lashing the broken mizzen

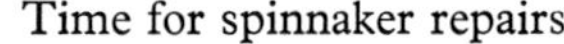

Time for spinnaker repairs

Heavy weather, the lee rail under

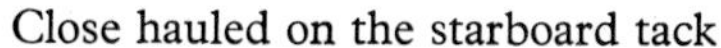

Close hauled on the starboard tack

Arrival at Sydney, with the Opera House and the Bridge in the background

A Christmas barbecue with Maureen in Sydney

At Sydney, the new mizzen mast being prepared, above; and, below, Pete and Robbie servicing the winches

Number 4 loose luffed and boomed out

Eric admires the view in Rio

Great Britain II's keel at Rio, showing the leak. The horizontal line shows where it has been ground off ready for repairs

Len, painting the deck at Rio

Great Britain II, first at the finishing line, Portsmouth April 1974

The trophies won by *Great Britain II;* from left, the author, Brigadier The O'Morchoe, Jack Hayward and Captain John Williams

right away. We tried the light spinnaker but a hole appeared in it so we had to take it down, a manoeuvre not helped by the pelting rain. Just when one was tempted to use rather fruity language the weather changed for the better; bright sunshine with quite a strong breeze. At last it seems to have settled down and we now have the reacher up. Everywhere below is soaking wet so this new combination of wind and sun gives us an opportunity to put our kit out on deck to dry.

The skipper is not too happy with our position because we have come about sixty miles too far south.

Robbie has been working on the radio aerial and he located the fault. The first boat we contacted was *Second Life* and Rod Ainslie gave us some very sad news. The joint skipper of *33 Export,* a guy I knew as Dominique, was washed overboard in a gale and they failed to pick him up. Apparently he was at the helm with his harness on, but a wave washed him out of the harness and over the side. He was a well liked member of the French crew and will be missed. If we ever need a reminder of how dangerous round-the-world sailing is, this is it. We knew when we set out that men could die during the race but I suppose we all cultivate a "well-it-couldn't-happen-to-me" attitude. We are all careful in everything we do and the size and ferocity of the sea make us aware of its threat. The two men who have drowned on this leg were experienced seamen and they were taken by the most daunting ocean in the world. This race is beginning to take its toll and in terms of men and yachts it will prove expensive. The skipper says that we must learn from Dominique's death and that all helmsmen when on Watch alone must wear tight safety harnesses.

Tonight we saw a fantastic sight, the Southern Lights. It is like a huge rainbow of white light and mist, varying in intensity and at times remarkably bright. Mike says he believes it is caused by a reflection from the ice cap.

Thursday, November 29th (John)
DAY TWENTY-THREE
Day's run: 245 miles.

An eventful night and morning. We rigged the pole up for a spinnaker but then the wind got up and we were hit by a number of squalls. We put the No. 3 Genoa up and boomed it out. On our next Watch the outhaul chafed through and we had to drop it. The wind was blowing at about 40 knots and no sooner had we re-rigged the sail than it chafed through again. "All Hands" was called to help get the sail in and I went on the foredeck to help Bernie. Suddenly a hank hit me on the head and knocked me clean out, how long for I don't know, but I awoke with a bad cut and a lump the size of a duck's egg. Alan did his Dr. Kildare bit and put a decent dressing on, but in doing so he had to cut away a lot of hair and it has left me with a big bald patch.

The lads said the cut was so bad that it warranted at least three stitches, but I was not at all keen to have Alan Toone poking around my brain with a bloody great needle and thread.

Radio communications are a complete mystery to me. The skipper tried to contact Melbourne this morning but in vain. We would pick up Portishead and Ostend, both on the other side of the globe, but we could not get a peep from Perth, which is only 500 miles away.

The wind is blowing about 30 knots apparent and we are really moving. The seas are huge and occasionally big chasms appear, maybe 30 or 40 feet across, looking like bottomless pits.

The cut on my head has done nothing to dampen my appetite and I enjoyed my lunch. Alan opened the last of the food packs and we made real pigs of ourselves with corned beef, peas, potatoes, then raspberries and cream.

Friday, November 30th (Chay) DAY TWENTY-FOUR
Day's run: 200 miles.

Light winds all day today. I saw a group of albatrosses gathering together on the water. It is supposed to forecast a spell of bad weather and although it sounds like an old wives' tale it may be right this time.

Saturday, December 1st (Chay) DAY TWENTY-SIX
Day's run: 170 miles.

Memo to self: Remember to listen to old wives when they start telling tales in future. We are now in the middle of a full 40 knot apparent gale being pounded God knows where. All this bashing and crashing takes me back to the *British Steel* days in this part of the world.

I have at last made radio contact with Melbourne. The bad news is that Tabarly is about a day ahead of us, though it is hardly surprising when one considers the damage we have sustained. The good news is that I spoke to Maureen who has just arrived in Australia with Samantha. It was wonderful to talk to her again and to hear that Jack Hayward had authorised a complete new mizzen to be flown out to us.

The helmsman is back to wearing goggles again and everything below decks is soaked.

John's head wound is much better.

Sunday, December 2nd (Chay) DAY TWENTY-SIX
Day's run: 170 miles.

I managed to take a sight and it was very disappointing. We have only made $5\frac{3}{4}°$ easting in two days, and normally we should have covered the distance in 24 hours. Our slow progress was due to the easterly gale last night and yesterday. We were tacking back and forth getting about 100 to 120 degrees difference in between tacks with a rig of No. 5 and No. 2

staysail. We had to run off a few times too and that didn't help. Then the No. 4 got jammed under the bow and it took us nearly two hours with all hands to sort it out. Everyone was soaked and fed up.

I had hoped to pip Tabarly to the post but it will be impossible now. If he has cleared Tasmania then he could have gone straight north, safe in the knowledge that we were tacking. Never mind, as a friend of mine is always saying, "It's all part of life's rich pattern".

After yesterday's gales today's weather has been a complete contrast, very light winds alternating with strong sudden squalls known as Line squalls or "Southerly Busters". In the late afternoon the winds freed and we were able to hoist the spinnaker. I hope this does not mean we are in for another gale. The Bass Strait is bad at the best of times but I would hate to be flying around there in naughty weather.

Same Day (John).

Eddie, Eric and me had a beard cutting ceremony today and the skipper was pleased with the result even if we were not. He certainly has a "thing" about hair. We tried to contact Melbourne again today but could not get through because of more aerial trouble. We learn lessons every day and one from this leg is that we should carry a spare aerial. We did pick up the tail end of a "strong winds" warning so we are probably in for some more ropey weather. We are all feeling the pace now and are looking forward to a rest in Sydney.

Monday, December 3rd (Chay) DAY TWENTY-SEVEN
Day's run: 202 miles.

Another gale, this time from the south-east and east. What a game! It managed to blow out the mainsail along a seam and John and Peter sat all day repairing it. John has been repairing sails continuously for 14 hours and has had only two hours' sleep in 24. We have been pounding into the gale and everyone is soaked to the skin. Alec got it worst when a wave broke over us and somebody—I think it was me but I would never admit it—had left the after hatch open. The gap was only about six inches but it was enough and Alec, his bunk, his sleeping bag and his change of clothing were soaked. It was truly the first time I have heard Alec swear, but he certainly knows all the right words.

We were pooped for the first time. We had to run off because the No. 3 sail was being changed and the water had sucked it over the side. A wave broke over the stern and I heard Bernie shout out; before I could enquire why I was enveloped in blue water. I felt the cold water lifting me and I grabbed blindly for the guard rail and a winch. Len left the wheel and grabbed my shoulder. It was over in a moment but once again the safety harness rule was emphasised. I am always going on at the chaps for not wearing theirs and this time I was caught out.

Tuesday, December 4th (Chay) DAY TWENTY-EIGHT
Day's run: 220 miles.

We sighted Cape Wickham Light at 23.00 hours. We had headed directly for it and our position when the sighting was made showed that our helmsmen had held good straight courses. We dropped the No. 3 which was boomed out and made some northing away from the Harbinger Breakers. I reckon we passed these reefs about two miles to seaward, which was quite close considering that it was night. Then, with the spinnaker up, we made for Wilson's Promontory, which is a headland sticking out into the Bass Strait. We made the passage well before dark and with good visibility and the wind astern, it was a relatively simple navigation exercise. It would however have been a different story if we had been forced to tack backwards and forwards in a storm such as we experienced the other night.

Cookie is turning out to be a great character. The chaps were getting on to him today about the length of time he spends sleeping. Anyone else would have either been hurt or angry with the criticism (totally justified!) but Alan is a real stoic. The comments just go in one ear and out of the other, he could not care less.

Wednesday, December 5th (Chay)
DAY TWENTY-NINE Day's run: 170 miles.

The winds have been all over the place and we find it frustrating having to tack back and forth, especially with such a short distance to go. Speeds have been low and with this East Australian Coast Current against us we will continue to make slow progress. I heard on the radio news that *Pen Duick* is due in at lunch time today and we will be in 24 hours later. Clever lads these reporters, they can estimate our time of arrival better than I can. The staggering thing is that if the Frenchman does beat us by 24 hours it is only about half-a-knot faster than us, or ten miles a day. He went a shorter route, his boat is definitely faster to windward and he has almost double the number of crew, so we cannot complain. Also—I nearly forgot—he has a mizzen mast.

Thursday, December 6th (Chay) DAY THIRTY
Day's run: 195 miles.

We have been tacking all day long. In 24 hours we have sailed about 150 miles and made 90 miles of forward progress. With the wrong wind and current it could be another 24 hours before we get in. If we get a calm we will be in trouble and of course all the time the other yachts are catching up.

Pen Duick is still not in and we have 140 miles to go.

I wonder where she is? What a finish if we were to pip him! It seems impossible but it might just be on; we listen to the news broadcasts from Sydney every hour and we are gaining.

We have started to clear up the yacht. Robbie has painted the main saloon out and it looks much better. Everybody has washed and scrubbed their bunk and bunk space. Fortunately the sun has been shining and the deck looks like a Chinese laundry. There is kit everywhere.

With the puffs today we have had the reefs in and out like yo-yos.

The more time we have on her, the better we are at sailing this yacht. At the end of the race we will just about be ready to get the best out of her.

Friday, December 7th (Chay) DAY THIRTY-ONE

We messed about with puffs of wind all night, tacking and getting nowhere. I suspect that at one time we were even going backwards. We heard on the radio that *Pen Duick* was definitely due in at 02.00 hours local time. That means she will be 120 miles ahead of us, half-a-day's run, or (taken over 30 days) four miles a day. I reckon that is a sixth of a knot.

Now is the time for reflection. I want to get my private miseries over before we reach Sydney and I see Maureen and Samantha. The truth is that we have done better, much better, on this leg. Nothing will alter the fact that Tabarly has come in first. I reflect on the things I could have done differently and my mind cracks with penance. The times we could have changed sail that little bit faster, or changed to a bigger sail, or gone further south or . . . There are a thousand little pinpricks, all of them covered by Kipling's *If*.

We crossed the finishing line at 04.46 hours, 50 seconds.

Tabarly beat us by just over eight hours.

PART FOUR

Sydney—Rio de Janeiro

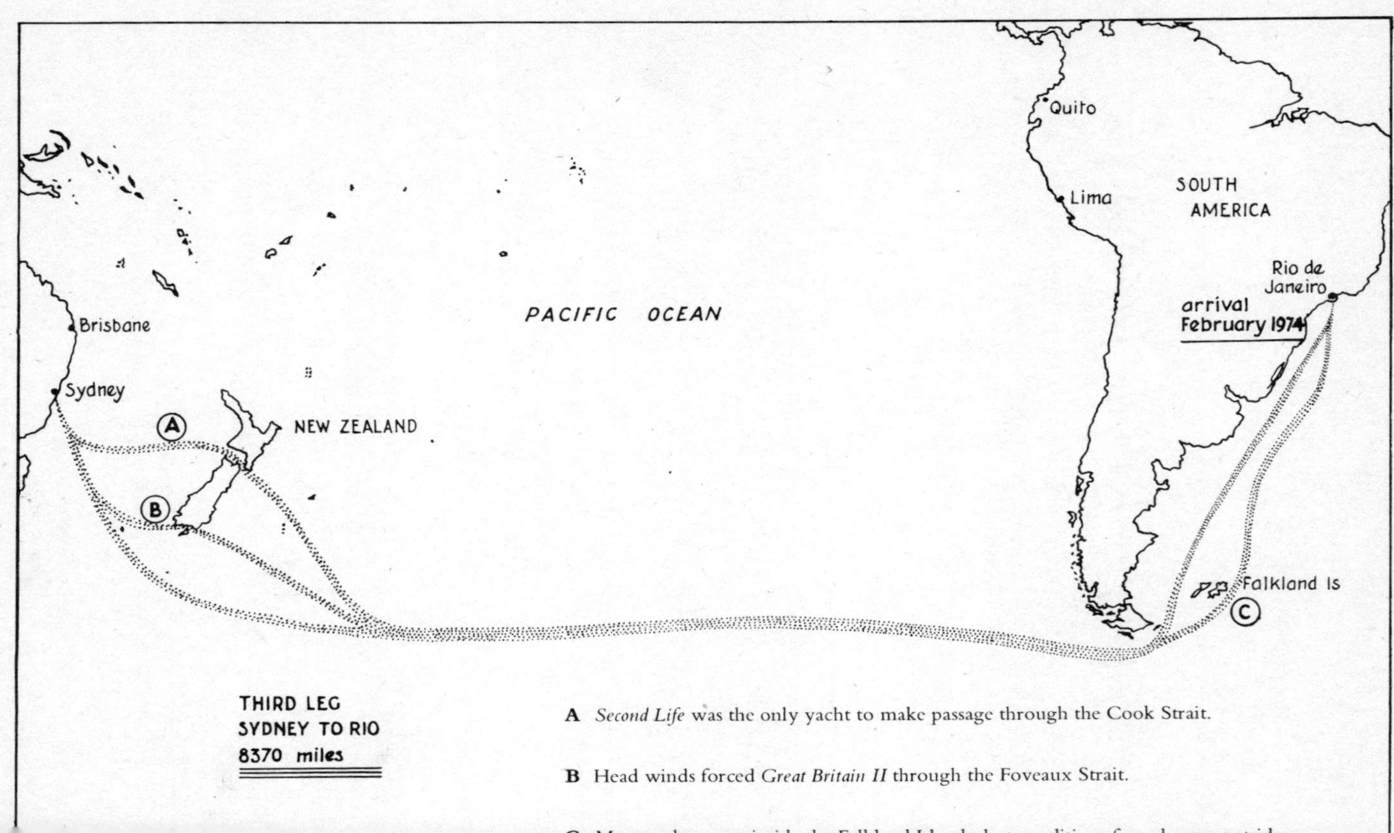
Quito
Lima
SOUTH
AMERICA
Rio de
Janeiro
arrival
February 1974
PACIFIC OCEAN
Brisbane
Sydney
A
B
NEW ZEALAND
Falkland Is
C
THIRD LEG
SYDNEY TO RIO
8370 miles
A Second Life was the only yacht to make passage through the Cook Strait.
B Head winds forced Great Britain II through the Foveaux Strait.
C Most yachts went inside the Falkland Islands, but conditions forced some outside.

8

SYDNEY IS A SUPERB HARBOUR. ITS NATURAL ATTRACTIONS have been cleverly combined with man-made facilities to provide a boating Mecca that looks as if it has jumped straight from the pages of a children's fairy-tale book. For me the big disappointment was the Bridge. Obviously very big deal in its day, the bridge is now relatively small compared with other similar structures. Having heard so much about it I suppose I was anticipating something much grander so my sense of let-down was more acute. The only good thing about it was that it had been built in Stockton-on-Tees, England.

Australians, particularly those living on the coasts of the continent, are orientated to boating but strangely this fact meant that the arrival of the Round-the-World Race yachts was not a momentous occasion for them. Of course Christmas was just around the corner and for yachting enthusiasts the imminent Sydney–Hobart Race held much more personal attractions. An additional diluting factor was that there were no Australian teams in the Whitbread Race.

Nevertheless we were made most welcome and once again

the round of parties and receptions started. After our experiences in South Africa, I had learned to trust every member of my crew completely and I can say with all modesty that I have received literally dozens of letters and messages of praise about the high standards of their behaviour and appearance in every port we visited. There were no problems therefore about the length or the intensity of the parties because the crew of *Great Britain II* were all paratroopers, which meant they could combine discipline with stamina even at a drinking party.

Mind you, this does not mean that the guys were little angels who did not enjoy themselves and occasionally let off steam. One yacht club incident was reported to me and although I was not there, I could not have influenced the proceedings if I had been. Apparently Len Price was there having a quiet drink with some friends when a stroppy member of the *Second Life* crew began to make disparaging remarks about the paras in general and the *Great Britain II* crew in particular. Len warned him but the guy, either because he was tipsy or foolhardy, continued to bait Len and his friends. The inevitable happened. Len hit the chap and then so I am reliably informed, bit his ear! The rights and wrongs of the situation were properly illustrated by the officials of the yacht club, who allowed Len to stay and slung the baddy out.

When I was told the facts next day I simply laughed. There were obviously going to be times when the restraint training we had practised in Scotland was not going to be enough, and this had been one of those times.

Eddie Hope's broken arm did not show any signs of improvement and the medics in Australia were firm in their recommendations that he should not complete the trip. Poor Eddie was naturally very disappointed but I could not afford passengers and the arm needed treatment so Eddie flew back to the U.K. Our crew was down to ten men.

We stepped the new mizzen mast, carried out other more minor repairs, and settled down to enjoy Christmas in the Antipodes.

The Blyth family were particularly lucky in Australia because they were befriended by a great guy called Lieutenant Colonel Stuart Peach. He had been 20 years in the Army and had served at least 15 of them in Asia. A remarkable man, he fascinated us for hours recounting his experiences and our friendship grew until he invited Maureen, Samantha and me to stay at his home for the rest of our time in Sydney. I am not a lover of hotel life, preferring the atmosphere and freedom of a home so we were delighted to accept. The move also saved me from near-bankruptcy because the prices in Australian hotels make the London Hilton tariff seem like that of Rowton House. Stuart lives with his mother in a lovely house overlooking Sydney harbour and our spell as guests there was the highlight of our visit to Sydney. We were able to celebrate Christmas with them and thus enjoy a traditionally family occasion. Parties were legion and usually take the form of barbecues, which is fine for the first few occasions but after a dozen barbecued meals in a week they begin to pall. I found myself dreading the thought of another stripy steak or crispy chicken portion and longing for shepherds' pie or haggis.

Life in Sydney is very Americanised with the majority living for the material pleasures of today. The pace is fast and the enjoyment almost frenzied. I found it difficult to join in with genuine enthusiasm, I felt they would do well to ponder on Wordsworth's lines: "The world is too much with us; late and soon, Getting and spending, we lay waste our powers. . ." This may be unfair because I have a confessed aversion to man-made pleasures, and my feelings were not borne out by a majority of the chaps, many of whom considered that Sydney was the highlight as far as ports were concerned.

Certainly the Aussies take their yachting seriously, although I was surprised not to see more big boats in the harbour. The most popular sailing dinghy is the Australian 16, which is crewed by three men who can use as much sail as they want in races. They are fascinating to watch and obviously men and boat generate a tremendous rapport. The Sydney–Hobart Race too is won as much by skill as equipment and as I watched the race on television I ached to be in there with them. I know that many of the Whitbread racers did enquire about taking part but because it was not due to finish until the day before our own "off" it was an impossibility.

There was a last minute panic among officials because some nutter had telephoned to say there was a bomb on board a British yacht. Like so many of these scares it turned out to be without foundation, but naturally they have to be checked so there was a slight delay with the start.

Saturday, December 29th (Chay) DAY ONE
Day's run: 103 miles.

We made a bad start. The start line was not at all clear and I could not line it up. Before the "off" the support crew from *Adventure* sailed over to us and threw an ominous round object on board *Great Britain II*. It was a melon with the word BOMB cut out of it. We had a good laugh about it and the incident well illustrates the camaraderie that has grown up between the crews.

We had trouble even before the start. While we were tacking backward and forwards I noticed a small tear in the sail. We whipped it down in double-quick time, Pete repaired the seam, and we rehoisted. We sailed for the line about one minute too soon which means that we had to sail along it and when the gun went we were at the leeward end with all the dirty wind.

It was Eric's turn this time: *Pen Duick* got off to a flying start!

Soon after the start we were left with just a zephyr of a breeze and it was interesting to see how the various yachts were performing. *Adventure* had taken a southerly course and appeared to be going well. *Sayula* overtook *Second Life* and then us. Then *Second Life* took us, we were not going to let them get away with that so we overtook them. They sailed hard and went past us again. It took us until dark to catch them and then we went flying past with our spinnaker up.

Same Day (Eric Blunn)

I was sorry to leave Sydney. It is a great place and I reckon I will be back. The only reason I wanted to get started was that we are now on the first of the homeward legs and I am on my way back to Peg and Elaine and the family.

Sunday, December 30th (Chay) DAY TWO

It seems that we are cursed with bad luck at the beginning of each leg. We noticed a small tear in the regular spinnaker so I called "All Hands" and got the storm spinnaker ready to peel. This only takes ten minutes but it was sufficient for an extra puff, increasing to about 30 knots apparent, to do the damage.

It blew the spinnaker centre right out and under the boat. The sail caught round the rudder and for safety's sake the only thing to do was to cut it. Len and Robbie cut it free and sadly we watched it go adrift and fall behind. That is about £1,000 up the spout, proving again that ocean racing is an expensive game.

We were too busy to feel sad for long so we cleared away and hoisted the storm spinnaker. No sooner was it up than we noticed a small tear that blew before we could change it. Luckily it can be repaired but with a second spinnaker blown in one night I was feeling angry. I have decided to take no more chances for a while so now the No. 3 is boomed out and the No. 2 staysail is being used as a mizzen staysail. It works well.

Monday, December 31st (Chay) DAY THREE
Day's run: 215 miles.

I phoned Maureen. Poor soul, she was trying to hold back the tears because it is Auld Year's Day and we are apart. Samantha was in good form though, saying "Over" when she had finished speaking. She picks things up quickly—when it suits her. I wished them both a guid New Year.

Bernie and I were changing from the No. 2 staysail to the No. 1 when Eric managed to pick up a big wave which threw me across the foredeck and down into the lee rail. Bernie tried to hold the sail but had no chance. The wave grabbed it and pulled it into the sea tearing the luff and also bending the stanchion over to 70°. John and Pete have got another repair job.

When we were rehoisting after pulling a reef in, the main halyard snapped so now we are using the boom topping lift as a jury halyard until the weather improves sufficiently for us to feed a new halyard through.

It is Auld Year's Night and regardless of how I felt I was determined to see the New Year in properly. I am the only Scot on board and the celebration is important to me. Eric and Alan made some fancy snacks and we all had an issue of two cans of beer and a double tot of spirits. At two minutes to midnight Alan went outside and as the New Year came he was our "first foot" below. We toasted the New Year with a drink from Alan's Ne'er Day Bottle and ate a piece of black bun that Frank Scott, my friend from Hawick, had thoughtfully sent to us. We wished each other a guid New Year and drank to absent friends, had a good yarn and retold a few jokes. It was not long before tiredness plus the thoughts of our families sent us all to bed—except of course the Watch. In the afternoon we opened our presents. Alan's wife Norma had sent all sorts of goodies and puzzles. She had obviously got most of us weighed up because she sent Pete a comic sex book. Maureen, funny girl, sent me a gardening book. Chris and Ruth Waddington sent a book of cartoons. John's family sent lots of goodies too and we must have looked a strange sight, nine paras all sitting round in funny hats trying to solve metal puzzles in the middle of the Tasman Sea with a Force 6 blowing.

January 1st (Chay) DAY FOUR
Day's run: 181 miles.

This has been the most memorable New Year's Day I can recall, but the memories are by no means all pleasant ones. We had planned for a major maintenance session during the light hours and it started with Bernie and Len reefing the main halyard. That may sound easy but the job takes over three hours because it is an internal halyard. The sheeves had to come out, messengers were sent up, and a weight dropped down the inside of the mast. It meant that Bernie was up the mast for the whole of the time and after a couple of hours he shouted down for us to clear the decks because he was going to be sick. We all dived below except poor Alec who had to stay on the helm and sure enough Bernie was violently sick. Three times he was sick and never once did I hear a word of sympathy from any other crewman. They are a hard lot. The only comment came from John who suggested to Alan that he should make Bernie another breakfast. I was secretly glad it was not me up that mast. I thought about the time when I was in *British Steel* and I had to go up in a Force 6, so I know it is not much fun.

Throughout the night the wind increased in puffs until at about 03.00 I decided to drop the regular spinnaker and peel to the storm. I called "All Hands" and we got the brand new storm sail up on deck but not out of its bag. Suddenly the wind increased dramatically and I gave orders to forget the storm spinnaker and drop the regular. No sooner had I spoken than the boat broached. I yelled into the dark for everyone to hold on but by now that call is a waste of time because the chaps know what is happening and what the priorities are. Eric had the helm right over but the main boom hit the water and the yacht pivotted on it rendering the rudder u.s. By the time the boom came out of the water it was too late. We had broached completely. If there had been time to think we would have been frightened, but here the only instinct was for survival, first of oneself and then one's comrades. Spray and great crashing waves broke across the yacht, incongruously sparkling in the illumination of the deck floodlight. Len was in the most imminent danger. He had been getting the new sheet ready and so was to leeward. I watched helplessly and I saw him wrenched off the foredeck, knocked and buffetted by the waves. I prayed he would be able to grab the guardrail but the next thing I saw was him being washed over the side. My stomach encompassed that sick, empty feeling as I realised that once he was completely over the side there was not a cat's chance in hell of finding him. The wave that had washed him over covered the deck for at least 10 seconds and possibly 20. I usually tend to play down a situation but make no mistake this was a bad one, I have heard them called rogue waves but I would call this one a real killer. After we had broached and the boat sat a little more upright miraculously Len came out of the water. As the wave swept him away he had become slightly tangled in the main boom sheets and he just grabbed blindly and held on. When we saw him he was over the side and well in the sea. Robbie, Pete, and I shot forward and yanked him bodily back on board. What a relief!

All the time that this episode was going on—I suppose the whole thing could not have occupied more than 90 seconds—hell was breaking loose. The regular spinnaker had gone into the water and was wrapped around the masthead completely in shreds. The mizzen spinnaker was blown (we found out later that hard work could repair it). Constantly there was the deafening banging and flapping of the sheets and sails as they were crucified by the 40 knot wind. The continuous hiss of the spray and the intermittent crashing of the waves on to the yacht made mad background music for the chaos being wreaked.

We dropped the main and the mizzen spinnaker. Then to make matters worse a heavy rain squall blew up. There was little more we could do in those conditions so I ordered everyone below to have a cup of tea and wait for the dawn. Only the helmsman stayed on deck and he was busy because even with just the rags of the spinnaker we were being blown along at about 5 knots and when we picked up a wave we shot forward at 7 knots.

Dawn brought the knowledge of the full extent of the damage. It took three hours to sort it out and one of the biggest jobs was caused by the spinnaker, which had wrapped around the masthead and smashed the Brookes and Gatehouse equipment, which meant that our instruments did not work. First we tied tell tales (ribbons) to the shroud to help the helmsman. As usual Bernie went up the mast, and after clearing the spinnaker and getting the bits out of the blocks, he changed the Brookes and Gatehouse so now we have instruments again.

When it was all finished and we were sailing relatively smoothly at between 10 and 12 knots, we went below where Cookie had prepared a bigger-and-better-than-usual breakfast. We deserved it.

Wednesday, January 2nd (Chay) DAY FIVE
Day's run: 215 miles.

We heard bad news today. *Kriter* told us on the radio that *Pen Duick* has been dismasted again. Eric did not deserve this sort of luck. He worked non-stop in Sydney, particularly on his mast, and the spreaders were sent off to be repaired because the ends were beginning to bend up. Eric will return to Sydney feeling dejected and frustrated as well, because all Australia is on holiday until Monday and he will have no chance of getting major repairs done. I meet a lot of yachtsmen who criticise and even dislike Eric Tabarly. I suppose it is understandable because he is undoubtedly the world's best ocean yachtsman and when you are king there are always those who will snipe. Personally I have tremendous respect for him and I am proud to be racing against him. I suggest that this latest disaster will effectively finish his chances of winning the Elapsed Time Prize and while I breathe a sigh of relief that our most threatening rival cannot beat us, it is still sad that his challenge should end like this. Knowing Eric however I suspect that this will not be the last time we race against each other.

I sent a telegram to Eric in Sydney. "JUST HEARD. OUR SINCERE SYMPATHY. GOOD WISHES FOR A SPEEDY RECOVERY. BLYTH & CREW".

This leg is beginning to take its toll. *Kriter* also told us that a crew member on *Tauranga* has a suspected broken back and they are going to have to drop him off at New Zealand. Someone—maybe the skipper—has broken an arm on *Grand Louis*. *Sayula* tore her mainsail.

Thursday, January 3rd (Chay) DAY SIX
Day's run: 220 miles.

We sighted New Zealand at 15.00 hours local time I decided to go straight through the Foveaux Strai and as the wind was from the south we would hav to come hard on the wind and beat to get roun Stewart Island. We passed between Solander Island an

South Island and it reminded me of the last time I was in this area, going the other way and beating hard in a gale.

At dusk I gave the Watch the position and a course to sail and told them I was going to bed and to wake me when we got near to Centre Island (we could already see the loom of its light). At 22.45 Alec woke me to say that the island was quite close. He was not kidding! It was about one mile away and I knew that just about 1½ miles to the south of it, precisely where we were, there was a dangerous reef. Before I could even mention the danger Len on the helm shouted: "Skipper, a reef, a reef." I shot on deck and saw about 30 feet away that the sea was white where the waves were breaking on the reef. It was decision time. I shouted to Len: "Go to port," then to Alec "All hands and life jackets". Next I dashed below and switched the radio to emergency frequencies. Back on deck again I told Len to go hard to starboard and after about five minutes the danger was averted. I gave the order to Stand Down. It had been a narrow squeak but laconic Len's only comment was, "You asked to be awakened when we got close. My close and your close are obviously not the same."

Sunday, January 6th, 1974 is a day that will live in my mind for ever. It started casually enough, quite a clear morning with the wind Force 5 gusting to Force 6. I decided to put up the heavy mizzen staysail to aid the 2,000-plus square foot reacher sail, the 800 square foot mainsail and the No. 1 staysail. In addition I said we would boom out the No. 3 loose luffed.

It was hard work and the chaps on deck with me, Eric, John, Pete, Bernie, Mike and Robbie, carried out the muscle-straining tasks with an efficiency that was almost second nature to them. They even had breath for a few ribald jokes at Pete's expense.

"Has the bird from Sydney phoned today?" Robbie asked him. "Only I thought I heard the phone going when I woke up."

"That wasn't the phone, that was wedding bells," said John. "I bet you promised to marry the poor girl. Anyway, what did the letter say?"

"What letter?" asked Pete, indignant and curious at the same time.

"The one that albatross brought this morning tied to its leg."

And so the banter went on and it seemed no time before we had got all the sails up and flying. Suddenly our world was shattered as John Rist shouted that dreaded phrase: "Man Overboard!" In such conditions it was almost unbelievable, but we all knew it was deadly serious because that is a cry never used in jest. "Luff up!" I cried. "All Hands!" At the same time I looked aft to glimpse a blue bundle being left astern in our wake. It was Bernie Hosking.

A lifebuoy was thrown after him immediately, the boomed out sail was dropped and then the mizzen staysail. We were trying to beat back all the time and the reacher sheet snapped, so down came the reacher. By now it was gusting Force 7 from the west and the men were working grimly and quickly. Our most experienced helmsman, Len, took the wheel and it seemed no time until we were on our way back. I directed operations while Alec plotted our courses. Our search took the form of a triangle course and we completed it twice before starting to tack back and forth in the area. Apart from essential orders no one said a word. Our ears strained for a sound or a cry above the noise of the sea. Time was against us. The water was 39°F, just seven degrees above freezing, and it was obvious that a man could not last for more than an hour. The minutes ticked away and although on two occasions we caught sight of the empty dan buoy there was no sign of Bernie.

After two hours I began to accept the dreadful fact that Bernie was dead. He could not have survived for that time in such seas. Still the search continued but in vain. I felt that empty nausea that grips you when you have been for a long time without food, and my limbs ached with dejection and sadness. Bernie was dead, drowned at sea. Only hours ago he had been with us on deck, smiling quietly at the jokes but never offering the cutting comment himself, content with his life on the sea and with his friends. He used his tremendous strength to make any task seem simple and he above all the others had shown a natural aptitude for sailing that in time would have turned him into an outstanding seaman. Given time Bernie would have been in demand as one of the best ocean crewmen in the game, but sadly Bernie had not been given time.

It was a grim and silent crew that formed the 'O' Group in the saloon of *Great Britain II*. How had it happened? Eric Blunn, our plumber, had seen the incident.

"I was waiting on the aft deck trimming the boomed-out No. 3 sail," he said. "There was a sail tie caught up with a hank and Bernie was attempting to release it. He was exerting quite a bit of force and suddenly the sail tie came away. Bernie lost his balance and fell overboard."

So that was it. Such a simple accident that had it happened at home we would not have given it a second thought. But at sea the slightest slip can cost dearly and now Bernie had paid the highest price of all. I sent telegrams to Terry Bond and the Parachute Brigade Brigadier: BERNIE HOSKING LOST OVERBOARD 6TH JANUARY 21.40 G.M.T. . . . POSITION 52°S 174°W . . . SEARCH NOW ABANDONED . . . PLEASE INFORM NEXT OF KIN AND RACE CONTROL . . . BLYTH.

Each member of the crew made a written statement about the incident and his knowledge of it, and these statements were produced at the subsequent court of enquiry in Rio.

At the 'O' Group it was obvious that the chaps were upset because Bernie had been our friend and now he was dead. But if his death was to mean anything they knew that they must face up to the loss and carry on in the race. They were paratroopers and death was not new to them. All had seen active service, some had seen their comrades shot beside them perhaps in a gutter by a stray bullet from a sniper's gun. They were not exactly used to death but it was not the same traumatic experience that it would have been for a civilian. We decided to press on to Rio. It sounds trite but it is true to say that it is what Bernie would have wanted. Death is a very personal thing and so final that there is little point in discussing it. We all had our own thoughts about Bernie but it was not possible to voice them to each other. Such a discussion would have been pointless. Alec Honey cleared and stowed Bernie's personal belongings from his bunk, we all went on deck and hoisted sail to push us on to Rio. I knew that Bernie would rarely be mentioned between us on the rest of the voyage and that such silence was a mark of respect for him.

Ironically, the tragedy of Bernie was followed by some tremendous sailing as we headed for the Horn. For a week we averaged around 260 miles a day and from our conversations with other competitors it was obvious that we were pulling away from the fleet. The chaps were a part of the boat now, able to hold their own against any other crew no matter how experienced the others were. We drove the yacht hard to take advantage of the winds, and in our urgency to complete this leg I took chances and inevitably they did not all pay off. For example, one day we had the reacher up as long as possible and the wind suddenly increased to 25 knots. The big sail blew and the damage was extensive, it meant days of hard labour for John Rist and Pete Bates. The winds and the waves were awesome. Blows of up to 45 knots were commonplace and the legions of waves were towering over 40 feet. With the reacher up we made around 12 to 14 knots but when we hit a wave right and surfed on its crest we could manage well over 20 knots.

This was sailing at its most exhilarating and its most dangerous. We all wore safety harnesses most of the time. We were beating, beating, beating into a Force 10 gale and the boat took a terrific pounding. On Thursday January 17th twenty-one days after leaving Sydney and less than a week away from the Horn, my log reads:

> We can now take stock of the damage caused by this constant beating.
>
> Three bulkheads are cracked, plus one bearer.
> One hanging locker is smashed beyond repair.
> Two shelves have been ripped away.
> One sheet has been chafed through.
> We have a very bad leak.
>
> The bulkheads being cracked are a problem because they slow our progress, but by far the biggest worry is the leak. I think it comes from the forward keel bolt. It takes an hour to fill the bilges and fifteen minutes to pump them out, so every Watch a man has to pump for a quarter-of-an-hour. The position is acceptable as long as it does not get worse. It has only to deteriorate slightly for us to be in a situation where we cannot cope. I have to be prepared for the worst so I will list the precautions I have taken.
>
> 1. Lifejackets have today been checked and are in position.
> 2. All survival kit has been checked and repacked (heliograph, flares, knife, compass, matches, paper, waterproof paper, tin opener, fishing kit, shark repellent).
> 3. Navigation kit has been listed and centralised.
> 4. 610 Lifeline has been checked and Alec, Mike and I have practised using it and familiarised ourselves again with the drill.
> 5. Jerry cans have been filled with water.
> 6. Boiled sweets have been packed together with tinned foods which contain juice.
> 7. Torches, batteries and first aid kit have been packed.
> 8. Air panels have been fixed.

9. Personal kit (small items such as wallet, cigarettes, and so on) has been packed

Places in the two life rafts have been allocated. I will be in the No. 1 raft with Eric, Peter, John and Alan. Alec will be in No. 2 with Mike, Len and Robbie.

It all sounds very dramatic but this is a very bad place to be and with this leak we are in a lot of trouble. It is better to be safe than sorry. It will be no use thinking of items we have forgotten if the yacht sinks.

That same day Eric Blunn's log recorded details of the leak, but he was also concerned about the cold. He wrote:

It's murder on the helm. The seas are hellishly rough and because we are hard on the wind we get a lot of spray. The water is freezingly cold. To make matters worse we have had to put out the tilley lamp because it is swinging about too much. This means that the helmsman has to put wet gloves on and his hands quickly become raw. Discomfort must be the mother of invention because I hit on the idea of putting polythene bags over my gloves and tucking them up my sleeves. It works a treat. My hands are warm as toast.

Mike saw me wearing the polythene bags. "I've got an even better idea," he said. "I know how to keep your face warm. Wear a polythene bag over your head." Nice chap, Mike.

The waves crash over the boat and you never know what damage they will do next. Tonight one of Southern Television's cameras was ripped by a wave from its mounting on the mast and lost overboard. Another wave did the same thing to the main compass cover. When you see just what power the sea has it must earn your respect. We are taking in water fast now. I pray the leak does not get any worse.

Someone must have been listening to Eric's prayers because after that initial crisis the leak did not get any worse. It certainly did not improve and we had to continue pumping every hour but at least we were in control. As we approached the Horn our daily progress slowed to just over 200 miles a day because the winds were comparatively light. We knew we were in the lead and the positions of the other yachts became less important as we pulled away from them. We wanted the Horn, the goal of every round-the-world sailor, and we wanted it fast. Temperaments became frayed as we knew it was only a few hours away and I attempted in vain to contact HMS *Endurance*, the survey ship stationed off the Horn. As we got nearer so things started to go wrong. We discovered that we had run out of diesel fuel. Goodness knows what had happened because we had stocked up sufficiently before we left Sydney. It could only have been a slow leak but whatever the reason it could not alter the situation. We started from Australia with 70 gallons, enough to give us a good battery charge for five hours once a week. Now we had five gallons in a can, which would give us one charge before Rio. Then our No. 1 staysail blew and quite deliberately I got ratty with Pete Bates.

"Pete, that bloody staysail blew three hours ago and it has just lain on the deck since then," I said. "It's your job to repair the sail and you are letting us all down by just leaving it. When sails blow I want work to start on them straight away." I knew that Pete would not take the criticism meekly, he is just not that sort of chap. He is a fiery fellow and it would not matter whether it was the Brigadier of the Brigade or the skipper of *Great Britain II,* if Pete thought he was being unfairly criticised he would say so.

He retorted: "I've been busy doing something else and I

work as hard as anyone on this boat. If you had wanted the bloody sail mended immediately you should have said so."

It was a flare up that could have amounted to insubordination but I had deliberately provoked it and had been strong in my comments because I wanted to provide an outlet for the simmering feelings that had built up in us over the previous days. The results of the row were, I am glad to say, exactly what I had hoped for. Pete started to mend the sail with a concentrated and furious dedication and he did not stop until the job was finished. By that time he had calmed down, so had I, and the incident had provided a talking point for the rest of the crew to take their minds off the frustration of trying to reach the Horn. Finally, it had obliquely reminded everyone that I was the skipper of *Great Britain II,* and that despite the friendship that had grown up between us all over the months, I was still capable of losing my temper and establishing my authority if there was not maximum effort on the boat.

Wednesday, January 23rd (Chay) TWENTY-SEVEN
Day's run: 235 miles.

> We have made contact at last with the survey ship HMS *Endurance.* We spoke on the radio at 14.00 hours and made rendezvous at 17.00 hours. It was great to see them again, just as it was two years ago in *British Steel.*
>
> They put up a couple of helicopters, one of which had Southern Television cameras on it, and then I spoke with the captain on the radio telephone.
>
> "Nice to see you Chay," he said. "I am not allowed to help you by suggesting a course but if you sail east for a bit and then turn left you should finish up in Portsmouth. My crew want to have a look at you so if you hang on we will come in close."

"Fine," says I. "Don't rush though because we must have time to put the fenders over the side. There's so much traffic in this part of the world that you might be forced in too close and scratch us."

The comment caused much hilarity in the radio room on *Endurance* because we were obviously the first signs of life they had seen in weeks at this bleak spot. They were even more amused when Robbie and Mike actually threw the fenders over the side.

They came in close enough for us to chat with the crew and to celebrate the meeting Len Price opened a bottle of champagne. He shook it first and when the cork blew we were all wetter than we had been since we left Sydney. It was a purely symbolic gesture though, because we had decided to postpone any celebration drinks until we had rounded the Horn and were out of the danger area.

At 21.50 hours we rounded Cape Horn. Now the chaps have joined the elite band of true Cape Horners. I have been round twice, once each way, and the way I feel at the moment that is my lot.

Same Day (Eric).

When I went on Stag Watch at 22.00 hours we were opposite Cabos de Hornos. It looks just like the skipper said it would, a barren and unmistakeable piece of rock, second to nothing in the world. I am sailing round the bottom of the world and realising an ambition I have had all my life. It is one of the most exciting things that has ever happened to me.

Thursday, January 24th (Chay) DAY TWENTY-EIGHT
Day's run: 220 miles.

We spotted Staten Island at 03.00 hours. The wind was against us so there was no chance of going through the Le Maire Strait. By noon we had cleared Staten

> Island and were all set for the Falklands. This evening I called the chaps together for a special Happy Hour.
>
> "You are now fully fledged members of the Cape Horners' Club," I told them. "The seas around here are relatively safe so we can afford to relax for an hour." We opened three bottles of champagne and finished them between the nine of us. I think we will all sleep well tonight!

And so we left the Westerlies and the cold Polar winds and made our way up the coast of South America to Rio. The weather got warmer but the sailing became much more frustrating because we were covering much less than 200 miles a day. In one 48 hour period we made a total of 273 miles and my impatience led to thoughts of being pipped at the post by some other yacht. The constant annoyance when you have not got good winds is that some other competitor on some other course has, and no matter what you do about it he will make up time on you. There is no use pointing out that when you have good winds the positions are reversed and he might be becalmed—I do not think that way.

Light winds bring their problems and this was graphically illustrated on the thirtieth day out of Sydney, when the wind dropped to nothing, and I went on deck with Pete and Eric to drop the spinnaker. The sail came astern and wrapped itself around the backstay. It was one of those occassions when nothing seems to go right and the more effort we made to free the sail the worse the situation became. Perhaps John Rist's recollection of the incident is the most descriptive:

> It took us all about four hours to free that bloody sail [he wrote in his logs]. The boat must have looked like a bloody circus act. There were blokes swinging from the main mast and from the mizzen and some trying to climb up the backstay. It really was one hell of a mess. Eventually Alan and Len managed to free it.

> We all panted a sigh of relief and all I could think of was thank God there was not too much damage to the sail. I've done so much sewing on this voyage that I feel like the old woman who lived in the shoe. Her problem must have been socks, mine is sails.

Another frustration was the lack of race information we received. We were now out of radio contact with most of the other competitors and although we knew we were in the lead, the information we picked up via radio programmes was so inaccurate that it was almost ludicrous. On January 27th we tuned into some channel that promised the latest news of the race and because we had just reported our position to Race Control I expected to hear a fairly sensible report. Instead the guy started off by saying: "Chay Blyth and his crew of novices are now beginning to get the hang of sailing. . ."

I am not a vindictive man but if the commentator had been on board *Great Britain II* I would have claimed the privilege of strangling him and I would have been the envy of every crew member. Then he added a touch of farce to his comic opera report by saying we would be in Rio within three days. I knew that with the best will in the world we were a week away and it was much more likely to be ten days before we landed. Such irresponsibility on the part of the media is to my mind disgraceful. You may feel that it does not matter but to me it certainly does, because first of all it reflects badly on us, as the public believes the report is based on information we have supplied. Secondly it confuses our families and friends, and our suppliers and sponsors. And finally it is untrue, which in my opinion is the worst sin of all, because once the news media start relaying blatant untruths the information system of which the world is so proud completely breaks down.

A highlight of the last few days before Rio was Cookie's birthday. Alan is one of the most remarkable men I have met, on the surface a quiet and shy character but at basic a man of many talents. In truth he was the only man about whom I had the slightest doubts before we set sail from Portsmouth. I thank my lucky stars that he came because he was a tremendous asset to the yacht. Alan is at once a poet, a philosopher, a maker of models, a writer, a wit, a sailor, and a wise man. My only doubt is whether he is a cook! Seriously, he had our respect on *Great Britain II* so his birthday on February 1st was quite an occasion. With great ceremony he lit a candle in the galley and then banned us all from there until dinner time. Although there was a mixture of exotic smells emanating from the cooking area throughout the day, no one dared ask what was being prepared because Alan had warned us that any questioners would be missed out at scoff time.

So it was with a mouth-watering sense of anticipation that we answered his "Grub's up!" call. We were not disappointed because Cookie had excelled himself. We had extra-hot curry, home-baked bread, apple pie and cream, home-baked jam tarts and cakes, all washed down with wine and champagne. It was delicious. Naturally some parts of the feast were more delicious than others. As John Rist said when he bit into the first jam tart: "Skipper, I think I have found something handy to stop up the leak."

The north-east winds varied between calms and Force 5 and slowly we progressed up the coast. Shorts came out of hibernation and our rests were again taken on deck. The constant ache of cold left us and we knew once more what it was like to crawl into a dry sleeping bag and to wake up warm. The fine weather encouraged movement and soon the crew were setting to work with a will on maintenance, repairs, and redecoration. Len and Eric washed the bulkheads where the tilley lamp had blackened them, then they took out the two life rafts and scrubbed their floors. Robbie rubbed down all the teak on the deck and then oiled it. Everyone played their part in the yacht's facelift, much needed after its weeks in the worst seas in the world. Surprisingly though, the change in temperature and the bustle of easy activity did not boost morale, but rather had an opposite effect. Perhaps the slowing down of our sailing progress was responsible but certain members of the crew were feeling low. Because they were paras they did not let their feelings show and to the outsider they were not noticeable, but my impressions of this time were reinforced after the voyage when I read their private logs.

For example, Eric Blunn wrote: "This sun is so unexpected and so warming that I have burned my shoulders in it and now must keep a shirt on all day. I am feeling quite miserable just lately, I don't know why. I think a lot about Peg and Elaine and I badly want to be with them again. I never realised before just how much my family means to me."

On the day following that entry an intriguing sentence from Eric's log emphasises the feelings. "During the spring-cleaning I had an argument with Pete and told him to watch what he called me or I would have a go at him." Just what Pete called Eric will be forever a mystery because when I asked them about the incident neither of them could remember it.

On February 7th, well ahead of the rest of the fleet, we took Line Honours at Rio de Janeiro.

PART FIVE

Rio de Janeiro—Portsmouth

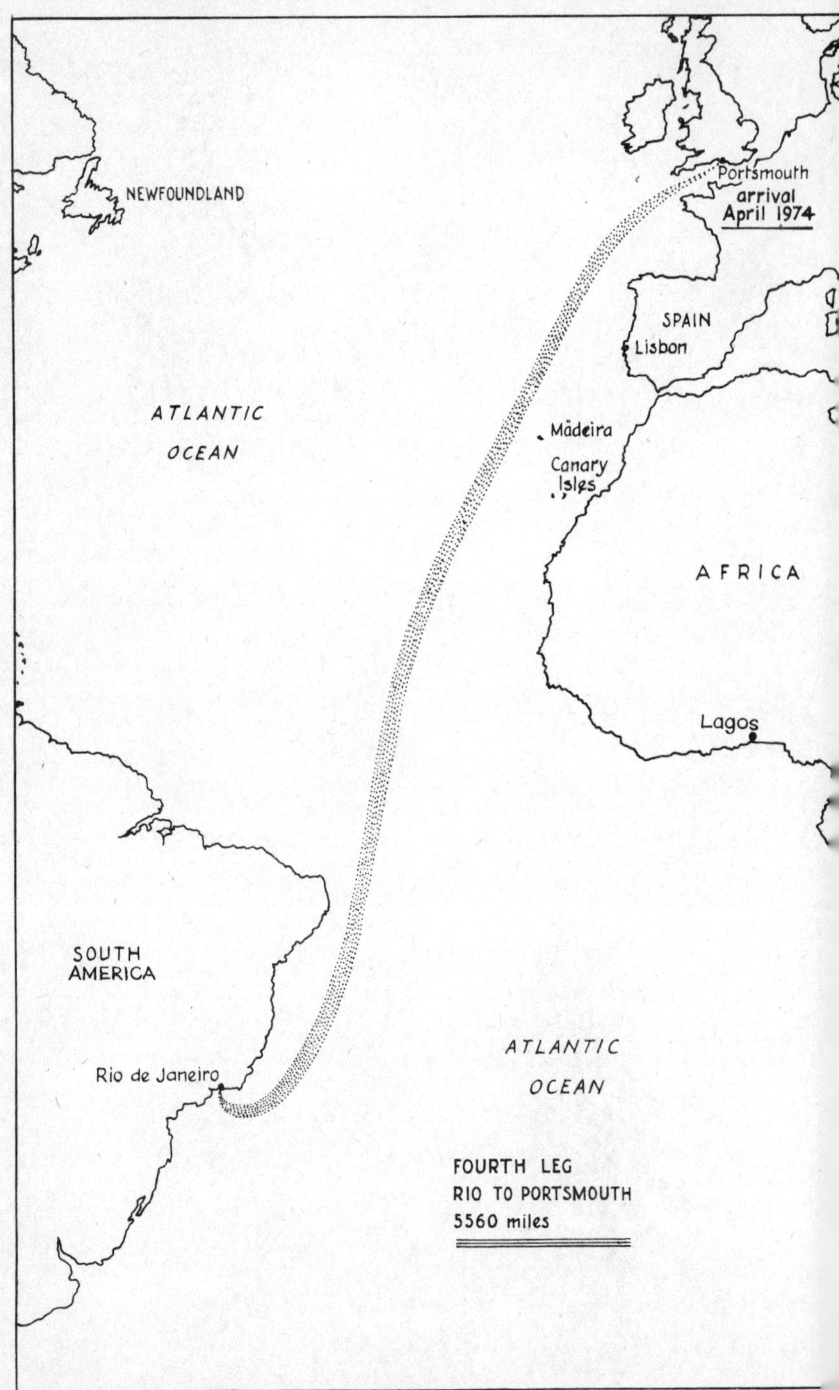

NEWFOUNDLAND
Portsmouth
arrival
April 1974
SPAIN
Lisbon
ATLANTIC
OCEAN
Mâdeira
Canary
Isles
AFRICA
Lagos
SOUTH
AMERICA
Rio de Janeiro
ATLANTIC
OCEAN
FOURTH LEG
RIO TO PORTSMOUTH
5560 miles

9

Rio de Janeiro is beautiful, exotic, unforgettable and filthy. From the harbour inland it is a sprawl with no overall plan. Examples of extravagant wealth stand alongside scenes of abject poverty and no one takes any notice because it is all part of the wild South American scene.

The seamanship in the Harbour is terrible. Predictably the Brazilians are speedboat-orientated and to them yachts are just big boats that cannot get out of the way quickly. Their sleek and ostentatious craft roar around the harbour careless of others and causing such a swell that our yachts rocked dangerously. The harbour itself is unclean—I always thought the Solent was murky but it is a perfumed pool compared to Rio. Even in the Inner Harbour which is dominated by one of the most exclusive yacht clubs in the world, the natives think nothing of throwing beer cans, paper, and sundry other rubbish into the water to cause further pollution. The yacht club is a marked contrast, big and opulent and costing thousands of pounds to join. We were delighted when the club's members and officials accorded us such warm and friendly hospitality. We had the use of the club facilities and after weeks of being confined with eight others on a 77 foot boat, it was like a collective birthday for us. Naturally we had to observe the rules which included not taking guests into the club and on no account taking a camera into the clubhouse on certain nights. Apparently the no-cameras rule dates from the time when a freelance photographer attended a function and avoided the usual screening when he left. The next day the local paper came out with happy snaps of local dignitaries whooping it up with young ladies who were obviously not on similarly intimate terms with the dignitaries' wives. Now security guards, burly and forbidding, make sure that expensive domestic upheavals are avoided.

Our arrival in Rio coincided with the carnival, a colourful pageant that goes on for days and is rather like the Munich Beer Festival, America's Fourth of July celebrations, Christmas, V.E. Day, and Guy Fawkes Night all rolled into one. It is a crazy devil-may-care time where natives and visitors live hard for today and feel terrible tomorrow. I am told that in two weeks of festival there are more than 100 violent deaths and having seen some of the happenings I can well believe it.

Personally such forced pleasures are not my scene so rather than wait for five weeks in Rio, I decided to fly back to Britain. There were several reasons for the decision and one was the high cost of telephone calls. Wherever I am in the world I try to telephone my wife at least once a day and my first call from Rio to our home in Dartmouth lasted forty minutes. By the time government tax and hotel tax and goodness knows what tax had been added to the exorbitant telephone charges, it was much cheaper for me to fly home. I also had some business to sort out and I wanted to cast my vote in the General Election.

Before I left Rio, however, I did have a chance to attend one of the festival highlights, the Hawaiian Night at the yacht club. The whole crew decided to go because although it was hideously expensive, it was a once-in-a-lifetime opportunity. We all wore sarongs and leis and we must have looked lovely. To cut down on cost we decided to smuggle in our own drinks (the local throat-scorching brew was about £12 a bottle at your table and pukka Scotch was around £20). The problem was the security guards who stand at every entrance and politely frisk all comers. We got around this by wearing an ingenious belt and slinging a bottle between our legs. We got the idea from Les Williams, who has been in Rio before and knows what to do with a bottle.

As the evening grew older and the Scotch bottles emptier so it warmed up. We had a reserved table alongside the huge swimming pool and next to the crew of *Burton Cutter*. Les Williams and his men are all great characters so we had a laugh-a-minute time. The staff and officials of the yacht club were immaculate as were the waiters in their starched white jackets, black trousers and bow ties. The walkway for waiters between the tables and the pool was only a few feet wide so inevitably the obvious happened—one of the *Burton Cutter* crew gave the slightest of nudges and the waiter carrying a tray with four full bottles of spirits went into the water. It looked like something from a Tom and Jerry cartoon and the waiter took it well.

The next man in was not so happy about it. I think he was a flag officer of the club, a man standing six feet and four inches dressed in black shoes, white socks, white shorts, white shirt, and a yachting cap with enough gold braid on it to put an American admiral to shame. I am not sure who tipped him in, but he certainly did not see the funny side of it. He came up grunting like a whale, his long hair over his eyes and his beautiful cap dripping over his ears. He was furious.

"Guards!" he spluttered, and two security men came rushing up to help him out of the pool.

"Arrest these men," he screamed, pointing at our combined crews.

Even the tough security chaps were rather taken aback by the impossibility of tackling twenty British sailors who were not going to come quietly, and the argument which followed was not helped by the fact that unaccountably the flag officer found himself back in the water.

Three times more the big man dragged himself out of the pool and three times more he somehow fell in again. In the end he decided that enough was enough, swam over to the other side of the pool and went quietly away.

★ ★ ★

Next day I forsook the fleshpots of Rio for a comfortable flight by British Caledonian back to U.K. It was wonderful to see Maureen and Samantha again. They recharged my energy batteries and I returned to Rio with just one aim in mind—Line Honours on the last leg. I knew that the handicap prize was impossible for us but more than anything else I wanted to be the fastest boat around the world. I wanted the Elapsed Time Prize.

★ ★ ★

When I assessed the situation before we left Rio it was a fair bet that we would be the fastest overall boat. I knew however that the real achievement would be to reach Portsmouth before everyone else and here was our major problem. The organisers in their wisdom had decided to start the boats off in four groups from Rio with a five day difference between the first and the last rated competitor. As scratch yacht in the handicapping system we, together with Les Williams in *Burton Cutter,* were the last boats to leave. The theory was that all the competitors would arrive in Portsmouth within a few days of each other.

We watched the official start of the first batch on Wednesday March 6th and it was one of the funniest sights I have ever witnessed. The Race Committee had dolled themselves up for the occasion in their Sunday best. They began the count down. The ten minute gun. Then the five minute gun. Then we got to the seconds—ten, nine, . . . three, two, one, BANG! There was not a yacht in sight. The sea was azure blue and deserted because not one of the first yachts off were ready. Eventually, three-quarters-of-an-hour after the gun went off, the first yacht glided over the line and at irregular intervals spread over several hours the others followed.

Two days later the second bunch set out and they provided a much more professional start, only *Tauranga* and *33 Export* were late. *Adventure, British Soldier,* and *Guia* crossed the line almost together and the Italian boat coped best with the light north-east wind.

Forty-eight hours elapsed and then we went out in *Great Britain II* to watch *Sayula, Second Life,* and *Kriter* start. Again the winds were light and *Kriter* was out-sailed, falling into a hole. *Sayula* was soon reaching and overtook *Second Life*. When they were out of sight I considered using the day as a dry run for our start, scheduled for the following day. I decided against the idea because the winds had dropped to almost nothing inshore and we had about eight guests on board.

Our actual start from Rio was farcical. *Burton Cutter* had engine trouble so we towed her out to the start line (if we had not done so she would have been at least two hours late). Even then half Les's crew were missing. A few minutes before the gun a speedboat came racing up with the baddies who had missed the boat. To make matters worse the start line was ambiguous. The rules stated that we had to leave a buoy to starboard and it was possible to do this without actually crossing the start line. *Burton Cutter* took this way out and made a good offing to windward. We decided that for the sake of a few minutes we would make absolutely sure so we started between the buoy and the shore triangle marks.

The wind was frustratingly flukey and we must have changed sails half a dozen times in the first hour. Eventually we settled for the No. 2 Genoa and settled down for the homeward run. The lads had mixed feelings about leaving Rio. Some of the more outward-going had been captivated by the atmosphere of the carnival city and the thought of going back to Blighty was not so attractive as it once had been. Others however (and I must admit I was among them) were looking forward to getting home. Typical of the feelings of those in the latter group were those recorded by John Rist:

> Rio was great but I am not sorry to leave. We know that home is soon to be a reality and because it is a non-stop sail away I have been keen to get started. Some of the chaps have been a bit unsettled about leaving because I think they are concerned that ordinary Army life is going to be rather a let down after what we have been through. We don't really talk about it in a direct way but I know it is going to be a wrench to all of us when we leave *Great Britain II*.

Typically, John could not remain philosophical for long. He has a tongue-in-cheek sense of humour that revealed itself in his logs time and time again. On March 13th he wrote:

> I'll be glad when we get some good weather so that I can dry my sleeping bag out. It has been wet since we left Rio. My bunk is without doubt the wettest in the boat, in fact the other lads call it the Swamp.
>
> We were hit by a number of squalls in the night and we all came up on deck for a shower. I had just got myself covered in soap and nicely lathered when the rain stopped. Just my luck.
>
> Alan cooked us quite a good meal tonight. Omelette, beans and potatoes. Fanny Craddock would have had a fit if she had seen it but it tasted O.K. Anyway, it makes a change from bloody curry.

It was about this time that we started "Think-Up" dinners We had very little variety of ingredients because provisions in Rio were so expensive that we relied on Army compo. Each man had to dream up a dinner menu using what we had got. Our entire food stock consisted of Pom, rice, spaghetti, stewed steak, a few vegetables and some eggs. It was generally agreed that Len's "Think-Up" was the most inventive. Assisted by Cookie he served hamburgers (no one knows quite what went into them), fried egg, fried Pom, and fried onions. It was beautiful.

We were sailing well and, although I am never entirely satisfied with a day's progress, I knew we were catching up and in some cases overtaking the fleet.

Tuesday, March 19th (Chay) DAY NINE
Day's run: 210 miles.

> We have had a good day's run but now, in the afternoon, the winds have become light. I picked up some positions on the radio and it seems we are doing well. *33 Export* is going like a train and they will be a problem. We have managed to catch up two days on them, thanks to our good start, and we have about 20 days to make up the rest. Factors that will influence the result will be the Doldrums and the route the various yachts take.
>
> *Adventure* has gone well over to the east. This is to make ground when they hit the north-east Trades. I am crashing north and worrying about easting later on. It seems most others are doing the same. *Guia* and *British Soldier* are really racing along.
>
> It's my turn to do dinner tonight. I am giving them fried rice with all sorts of stuff chopped up and shoved in. It doesn't look too bad but the rice is cheap wog stuff, not American long grain. Never mind, it will be a surprise because they all assume I will dish up another curry.

Wednesday, March 20th (John) DAY TEN
Day's run: 121 miles.

Fairly calm night with hardly any squalls; in fact we were almost becalmed a couple of times. The wind finally picked up this morning and remained constant. During the afternoon we had to drop the No. 2 Genoa and put the reacher up. Then the wind rose again so it was back to the No. 2.

Over the past couple of days we have noticed a few small flies on board. Alan, being in charge of hygiene, had thoughtfully bought a fly spray in Rio. The trouble is, he bought disinfectant instead of insecticide. The result is that we have the cleanest and healthiest swarm of flies on the high seas.

Eric got a Black Star today. He managed to lose our only bucket overboard. He and Len spent the rest of the day trying to make a temporary bucket out of sailcloth.

Alan is making a super model of *Great Britain II*. He has almost finished it but is taking it with him wherever he goes because Len has threatened to see if it floats.

Big event of the day was me having a haircut. I look much better and ready to knock 'em dead in Portsmouth. Some of the other lads are not too pleased at the prospect of having to cut theirs though—they rather fancy themselves with flowing locks.

Thursday, March 21st (Chay) DAY ELEVEN
Day's run: 125 miles.

We heard on the radio about the nutter who attempted to kidnap Princess Anne. It is a good job he did not succeed and an even better job that they caught him. If not he would have had nine very angry paras—us—on his trail as soon as we got back.

Saturday, March 23rd (Chay) DAY THIRTEEN
Day's run: 200 miles.

The starboard running backstay winch is being pulled

forward. Robbie noticed it first. We dropped the staysail in a hurry and then Robbie stripped the winch. Two stainless steel bolts had sheered through metal fatigue. Also, one of the stainless steel strands had broken on the running backstay. Fortunately this time we had replacement parts and were back to normal quite quickly, but we will have to watch these things in the future.

There are other troubles too. The mast appears to have gone forward a bit so Mike and Alec shoved another 1,000 lbs. on the hydraulic backstay. The hydraulic really has been a godsend. Every knowledgeable yachtsman who comes on board *Great Britain II* is immediately drawn to it. I must remember to thank the National Engineering Laboratory when we get back because they have done a great development job.

Sunday, March 24th (Chay) DAY FOURTEEN
Day's run: 190 miles.

We changed to the No. 3 early this morning and as we dropped the No. 2 the wind caught it. One of the hanks flew free and hit Len just above the eye. It was a nasty cut but after Cookie had changed hats and become the medic it seemed O.K.

We have just learned some very bad news. Mike went to shove a charge in the batteries. He discovered the engine would not fire and the batteries were flat. It will cause chaos. Because the leak has opened up again we will have to pump by hand from the main bilge. We have no emergency radio, no lights (only fifteen candles). We are also without navigation lights and that's the one I don't like. We have only our emergency lights and they may not last. It is all right when you have plenty of sea room but not when we are closing the Channel with all its shipping.

These race reports get dafter! We heard today on the commercial radio that *Burton Cutter* is second on handicap and we are second from last. We know that we only have to give them half-a-day on this last leg and we also know that we are more than a day ahead of them. The same applies to *Adventure*. We knew from position reports that she is behind us and that we have gained three days from Rio. We are not halfway home and as we only have to give them five-and-a-half days on the whole leg my schoolboy arithmetic means that we should be ahead of them on handicap. Not so. The race organisers put them fourth. It is farcical really, but for us competitors it is also frustrating, because we can never know with any certainty how we are doing. It's not just me. Think of poor *Guia,* rocketing along but according to the powers-that-be she is way down the list. I think I will stick to my original intention of Elapsed Time Winner and Line Honours, they are easier for my pea-like brain to calculate.

Monday, March 25th (Chay) DAY FIFTEEN
Day's run: 192 miles.

Robbie, Len and John have spent all day trying to fix the electrics. But the lads are working in vain because try as they might the juice is just not sufficient to turn the engine.

Meals have been brought forward to take advantage of the light. Breakfast is at 07.30 hours, lunch at noon, and evening meal at 17.30 hours. Lights out (or to be more accurate, candle out) at 22.00 hours.

Tuesday, March 26th (Chay) DAY SIXTEEN
Day's run: 193 miles.

Good news—the engine is working.

Bad news—the speedo and log are useless.

Len and Cookie worked all day putting the batteries in "series" and when they had finished there was a total of 48 volts available instead of the normal 24 volts. All the while they were setting the thing up there was a succession of sounds and smells that I can only relate to burning. When I expressed alarm Cookie reassured me:

"Don't worry, skipper. We know what we are doing. You always complain when I burn things. But you should be used to it by now."

When everything was set up they gave it a quick flash—and I use the word advisedly—and the sea lit up for miles around.

"Maybe that's a little too powerful," said Len with masterly understatement so they reduced the power to 36 volts. Cookie used his fly spray gun to force ether into the manifold and then they gave it a burst. BANG! The explosion all but took the head off the engine but all's well that ends well and we now have power and hence light.

Same Day (John).

I always knew that fly spray gun of Alan's would come in handy. Mind you, the explosion shook us all. It seems the only things safe from the gun are the flies. It's great to have light again. On Night Watch I don't end up with my dainty size 8 feet in Pete's clodhopping size 10 sea boots.

Wednesday, March 27th (Chay) DAY SEVENTEEN
Day's run: 190 miles.

We fixed flares to the lifebuoy and I gave a safety talk on the perils of the North Atlantic. No swimming, and be always alert.

It should have been a big celebration today because it is Mike's 29th birthday. Cookie made special cakes and they were terrible. Nobody ate them. The remarks were unrepeatable but Cookie just smiled at the funny ones and scowled at the crude ones. Then Alec tried to save the day by producing a bottle of wine but that was too foul. In the end we decided on the usual—curry.

We changed to the second water tank today. The water is evil. You are not supposed to drink the Brazilian water and that is where we filled up. If you have ever tasted it you can understand why they warn you off. Cookie says he always boils it but sometimes I wonder.

Scrabble is the latest time-waster. Maureen gave me a set for Christmas and everyone enjoys the game. The other leisure time activities are chess, reading and, most popular of all, sleep.

Friday, March 29th (Chay) DAY NINETEEN
Day's run: 192 miles.

Very light winds and sunshine all day. I had a bath, shave, and change of clothes and I feel much better. Everybody's going in for a panic tan and a big slim. The feeling of closing with Blighty is coming on us. The crew watch me put our daily noon position on the chart and they are taking a much keener interest than usual in the day's run.

We will lose the north-east Trades in a couple of days and go through the Horse Latitudes. We are all hoping it will be like our passage through the Doldrums—straight through without much trouble. I tried to contact the other yachts today but had no luck. It is most frustrating. When I don't know I always expect the worst.

21.30 hours. I have just watched the chaps put a reef in the main and they really are good. From the moment I gave the order for the reef not a word was spoken until the job was finished, and John shouted "Sheet!" to trim the sail.

It will be a sad day when we disperse. I know I will never again get a crew that is so fit, so well organised, and above all so loyal. They have given me and *Great*

Britain II twelve months of their lives. I hope we have done our bit for them.

Saturday, March 20th (Chay) DAY TWENTY
Day's run: 187 miles.

The noon sight and chart mark up has become the highlight of our lives. Everyone asks "How far have we come?" We can't get back to Blighty quick enough. Our days are spent concentrating entirely on speed and sail trim.

We all had a whirl at maintenance today. Robbie tried to sort out the navigation lights, which were not working. John and Len organised the exit boxes for halyards. Eric fixed a new tap on the pump for the bilge. Cookie stripped the cookers and cleaned them. Pete oiled the skylight screws. Mike checked the engine and controls which were jamming. Alec gave Len a helping hand and also pumped out. I had another go at the radio.

It's getting colder now. We have all forsaken our shorts in favour of sailing trousers. On Watch at night we wear pullovers and jackets.

I just got very ratty with Pete. He was on deck and slipped because he was not wearing shoes. "This is the third and last time I will tell you," I shouted. "It's bloody dangerous to go on deck without shoes." Apart from anything else he could have damaged his feet. We are in the North Atlantic and the sea here can be vicious.

And so we battled on towards Portsmouth, sailing hard o gain the ultimate triumph of Line Honours. Sometimes he winds were good to us, sometimes not so helpful. lways we forced the yacht through the water, each man vith his private thoughts of what the future held in store or him. Naturally we talked among ourselves and discussed our plans, but so much had happened in our months at sea, we had learned so much about the world and about ourselves, that we knew we were changed people and we could never return to being the men we were before.

Friday, April 5th (Chay) DAY TWENTY-SIX
Day's run: 187 miles.

Our distance today was rather disappointing when compared to yesterday's excellent 250 miles. We have been listening to the race positions on the World Service of the B.B.C. but the whole thing has become laughable. They said that *33 Export* was in the lead and *Burton Cutter* was doing well. Naturally we were nowhere. Personally I think the Race Committee, who are all very nice guys, are giving every yacht a turn at being first.

We have not got a log any more. The spinner went last night. The usual story is that a shark got it but honestly it could have been anything. The shark story sounds better but I prefer not to tell lies in case the sharks decide to get their own back by having a go at me.

We are trying to average 200 miles a day so that we will get in by Wednesday, but one calm and we have had it. Today's run was not bad I suppose, considering we have had light winds and a heavy swell. I fear the spinnaker took a bashing, so did the mizzen staysail Never mind, we have got to get there.

I had an 'O' Group this afternoon. Without being too obvious about it I told the crew that they should consider their appearances because the eyes of the world would be on them in a few days' time. We are beginning to sort our kit out and clean up the boat a bit Everyone had a good wash and a change of clothing too, although we plan to have more of both when we get off the Isle of Wight.

Wonders never cease. Robbie has had a haircut. He was beginning to look like that dog in the paint advert on television. Like Cookie, he has been making a model of the yacht and it is quite good. He plans to give it to the first wee boy he sees when he steps ashore.

Saturday, April 6th (Chay) DAY TWENTY-SEVEN
Day's run: 240 miles.

Success! I managed to contact Portishead Radio today. I phoned Maureen and the line was clear as a bell. It was great to talk to her again. Apparently Samantha has had flu for the past ten days but she is fully recovered now and will be there to meet us.

I also spoke to Tony Holden and he really cheered us up. He says we are about 300 miles ahead of *33 Export* and they are our nearest rivals. *Adventure* is in there somewhere but we're not quite sure where. Tony says if we get in on Wednesday—I think it's a vain hope—then we will have beaten the old Clipper Ship record. It looks more likely to be Thursday, which will equal the record of 144 days at sea. This sort of information should spur us on to put more effort into the sailing but there is no point in me asking anything more from the chaps. They are giving maximum effort for the whole of the time.

We got B.B.C. Radio Two for the first time. Guess who? "What's the recipe today, Jim?"

"Well, I am very glad you asked me that Raymondo because today we are going to titillate the ears of the good ladies with a super dish called curried rice pudding, sent in by Annie Bloggs of London. . ."

Even though you are away from Britain for several months there are some things guaranteed not to change. I had hoped that Jim's recipe would inspire Cookie to greater things. No such luck. Stew again for lunch.

The wind is gradually backing to the north. It is the north-east that we don't want.

Sunday, April 7th (Chay) DAY TWENTY-EIGHT
Day's run: 190 miles.

The clocks have been put on to British Summer Time and there has been fog for most of the day. Now we know we are nearly home!

The bad news is that we have lost the last of the spinners—those bloody sharks again—so we will have no log for going up the Channel. Not to worry, Columbus did not have one either.

We have just heard on the B.B.C. World Service that we are leading on handicap. It does not fill us with any great joy because we do not know whether to believe it. On the last World Service report we heard that we were lying eleventh and that was a load of rubbish so there is no reason to believe that today's news is any more accurate.

The awful news is that we are being headed so we are having to tack. It is desperately frustrating at this stage of the game. There is a high pressure over Scotland and that is what is causing the trouble. It is annoying to think that everyone in Britain will be having glorious weather while we are crashing to windward getting nowhere fast. The old imagination is starting to work again and I can picture the other yachts with Westerlies catching us up. I had hoped to make Portsmouth by Tuesday night or Wednesday but it looks like Thursday now. Damn this bloody wind.

Monday, April 8th (Chay) DAY TWENTY-NINE
Day's run: 135 miles.

Most of the day it has been foggy and the wind has been up and down like a bloody yo-yo. We keep saying "Not far now," and "Soon be home," and similar daft things to each other but the fact is that this last bit is the most frustrating and annoying because it is such a drag. One thing that brightened our day was a visitor. Eric was on the helm and most of us were down below when the constant noise of the sea was broken by a drumming thunder.

"Nimrod!" shouted Eric and we all dashed up to wave to the plane.

I guess it was from RAF Mountbatten at Plymouth. How the hell he found us in this lousy visibility I will never know. He must have some good aids in that plane. While the Nimrod was going round the wind dropped again so we dropped the No. 2 and put up the No. 1, took a reef out of the main and hoisted the ensign. We dipped the ensign to him as he went past and in return he flew his last sortie over us and switched on his landing lights. We waved, and he climbed steeply away and disappeared. It was all very exciting.

We still have 380 miles to go and we are getting nowhere fast. The wind is still north east. It is unbelievable. We only made good 135 miles today although we probably sailed 180. We might get in on Thursday morning but that seems doubtful now because the wind is dropping again!

Tuesday, April 9th (Chay) DAY THIRTY
Day's run: 120 miles made good in 21 hours.

We tried to contact Land's End Radio but it was no go. The M.V. *Sorrento* called us and offered to relay a message so I asked them to let the Race Committee know that my E.T.A. was 15.00 hours on Thursday.

Soon afterwards I tried Land's End on the off chance and surprisingly got through. I spoke to Maureen and she told me that everyone was biting their nails with the waiting at Portsmouth. God, we will be glad to get back. This race has been hard especially with such a small crew—numerically that is. To me they will always be the biggest men I will ever know.

My other calls were to the *Daily Mail* and the B.B.C.

Somebody interviewed me for the "Today" programme and his first questions were what had we missed during our time at sea and what were we looking forward to doing when we got home? As John Rist said, after six weeks in all-male company those questions seem a bit superfluous.

Wednesday, April 10th (Chay) DAY THIRTY-ONE
Day's run: 102 miles.

We are getting close and everyone is getting very tense. I can feel it and I can see it. We had the first major row of the trip between two of the crew members. I won't say who it was between or what it was about. Suffice to say it was all over and forgotten in a couple of minutes.

I called an 'O' Group this afternoon. The chaps were expecting it and I think most of them knew what I was going to say. First, I thanked them for making the trip and for playing their individual parts in the success of the voyage. I found it quite difficult to put into spoken words just how grateful I was to every one of them, and I find similar difficulty writing it down now. They knew what I meant and they made it easy for me with a few sympathetic but unrepeatable interruptions. Then I got down to the nitty-gritty.

"We are nearly home and we shall soon be going our separate ways," I said. "One thing is certain. We are not the same chaps who sailed from Portsmouth. We have seen things and done things that have changed our lives and our attitudes. We will never look at things in quite the same way again. We have tasted the good life in ports and we must be careful not to let it go to our heads.

"Confidences have been shared and we have spoken to each other about feelings that would normally never be shared. It is important that we continue to respect these confidences once we have gone our various ways

"Because you will soon be leaving *Great Britain II* this does not mean that she will be going out of your lives altogether. She will always be part of us. Although at times she has been a bit temperamental and has given us our fair share of troubles she is a great yacht and she has more than done her job as far as we are concerned. So when you are telling people about the voyage never be unkind in your comments about *Great Britain II*.

"And when you do tell people about the trip make sure you tell a complete story. Tell them about the good times as well as the bad, the fun as well as the frights.

"In a few hours we will be home and all the ballyhoo will start up and they will be saying fantastic, fantastic, and you will be interviewed on television and in the newspapers and if you are not very careful you will begin to believe that we are all Very Special People. It just is not true. Never ever believe your own publicity. In a few days we will be forgotten by the public and in a few weeks you will be back at your jobs in the Paras. In a few months even your friends and families will rarely mention this trip. So prepare yourself for the fact that we are about to become Nine Day Wonders."

That was quite a speech and I had thought carefully about it. It can't begin to prepare the chaps for the changes they will be experiencing in their life styles, but I had to make some effort because I was the person responsible for choosing them to come on the trip.

* * *

As we approached Southsea the excitement was tremendous and a flotilla of craft of all shapes and sizes came out to greet us. The crew's wives had made banners saying WELCOME HOME *GREAT BRITAIN II*, and everyone was waving Union Jacks.

At three o'clock on the afternoon of Thursday, April 11th, 1974, flying her spinnaker, *Great Britain II* crossed the finishing line at Southsea. As we lowered the spinnaker and the gun went to signify the end of 144 days at sea we were hemmed in by dozens of boats. The crew's wives, children and girl friends were all on one boat and I suspect there were quite a few open tears of pleasure from them, and maybe a few hidden ones from us as we sailed in unison to land. For the women it was the end of an ordeal that has in its way been equally as hazardous as for us. Now they cheered and waved and wept with thankfulness that it was at last all over.

Many of the other boats contained the people who had done so much for the *Great Britain II* venture and who had been a source of inspiration to us. Maureen and Samantha were with Chris and Ruth Waddington in Chris's launch. Jean and Jack Hayward, with Rick and Jonathan, were in a speedboat with Carol and Terry Bond and Chris and John Wright. There were scores of other friends and relatives. It was a tremendous homecoming, a day we will remember for the rest of our lives.

It was the eve of Good Friday and the Bank Holiday crowd had already begun to arrive at the South Coast. Although we had tried to prepare mentally for the reunions, it was still an emotional affair as we docked at H.M.S. *Vernon*. The Race Committee welcomed us, the champagne flowed freely, wives and children and aunties and uncles and cousins and friends and the Press and television and people who had no right to be there at all, but just wanted to join in came on board. Jack and Jean Hayward were there with their family, and the Brigadier, and my friends from Hawick, and a Parachute Regiment band was playing away and there was kissing and hugging and back-slapping. Reporters were asking inane questions, men with tape recorders were wanting a few quiet words, television directors were draping microphones round our necks and jamming light meters against our noses.

It was the best kind of chaos where everyone was

enjoying themselves and we could bask for a short while in glory that we had not asked for, but which was thrust upon us.

I had experienced it before so I knew what was coming. I was determined to keep my cool, answer as many questions as possible, and as soon as everyone was happy Maureen, Samantha and I would slip quietly off to an hotel for our private family reunion. I have an aversion to showing emotion in public. Affection is a personal feeling which cannot be truly experienced in front of a crowd of onlookers. To my mind, men who are forever fawning over their wives or girl friends in public suffer from a feeling of insecurity and are falsely compensating by showing off.

Only minutes after we docked, we were interviewed live on Southern Television. The interviewer was talking to Jack Hayward and me about the trip. "What is going to happen to *Great Britain II* now, Mr. Hayward?" he asked.

"You'd better ask Chay," replied Jack. "I've just made a present of the yacht to him."

That evening at the Havant Albany Inn at Hayling Island, Jack laid on a Welcome Home dinner for the crew, plus their families and a few friends. It was a grand climax to the trip, a completely informal occasion where we were able to wind down away from the prying eyes of the Press and the public. The speeches were short and to the point and by far the best was that made by Jack Hayward.

"I am delighted that *Great Britain II* has been so successful," he said. "And I am delighted that my faith in her and Chay has been justified.

"But the real triumph belongs to the linchpins of the whole venture. The crew. Theirs is the glory."

Postscript

AFTER A WEEK'S LEAVE THE CREW GOT TOGETHER AGAIN TO tidy up the yacht. Already the voyage was a memory and the complications of land living and the future were clouding and distorting their feelings. Before the world enveloped them too much I was keen to know the answers to a few basic questions, but I felt that because we had enjoyed a skipper—crew relationship their answers may have been guarded if I had asked the questions direct. Therefore my friend Terry Bond talked privately to each crew member. Here are their comments, good and bad.

LEN PRICE

Q. Did you enjoy the trip?

A. Yes. It was different from what I had expected and it would not be fair to say that I enjoyed every minute of it. The second leg was by far the roughest as far as weather was concerned, although we had anticipated the run between Sydney and Rio would be the worst.

Q. Do you think the crew got on well together?

A. We got on O.K. together. Obviously on such a long

trip we were bound to have differences of opinion but our training in Scotland had taught us how to deal with aggro. We would walk away from it and we would forget it. The secret is never to bear a grudge. I reckon our crew was the most compatible. There was trouble on many of the other yachts and I got the impression that the biggest problems were on the French boats.

Q. What are you going to do now?

A. I hope to get a posting to a yacht club as a sailing instructor again. I have been an instructor for three years and I want my future to be tied up with sailing and the sea.

Q. What did you think of Chay as a skipper?

A. He was O.K. I probably have more criticism of him than anyone else in the crew because I knew something about sailing and there were things that he did that I would have done differently. But there can only be one skipper and you have to put up with his peculiarities.

Q. Which port did you enjoy most?

A. Sydney. I had relatives living about 120 miles outside the city so I spent a fabulous Christmas with them.

Q. Are you at all worried that life will be a bit dull now?

A. It will be dull but I accept it and it will not worry me. When you are in the Army you are adaptable and I will soon get into a new routine. As long as I can stay with boats I am not too worried.

Q. Would you do it again?

A. Yes. I want to.

Q. Were there any disappointments for you?

A. Yes. I thought the medals that Whitbreads gave us at each port were rubbish. I got better prizes for coming third in the high jump at school.

MIKE THOMPSON

Q. Would you do it again?

A. Yes. I would start again tomorrow if I could.

Q. Was the journey what you had expected?

A. Not really. It was not as frightening as I had anticipated, probably because of the boat. Because of the sheer size of *Great Britain II*, we were not as affected by the big seas as some of the other yachts. We had some fabulous experiences too that I could not have anticipated beforehand. When the yacht was surfing for instance it was the most exhilarating thing that had ever happened to me.

Q. Which port impressed you most?

A. Sydney. I like the people there and I like their approach to life. Maybe they are a bit blunt and abrupt at times but at least they mean what they say.

Q. Were there any disappointments for you?

A. I suppose the only disappointment I can recall is a rather negative one. Before we set sail I was rather apprehensive about my personal reactions to the really big seas and rough sailing. I had never experienced either and so I anticipated a feeling of fear. But when the going did get bad I found I was totally in control of myself. At no stage was I ever frightened so that is an emotion I have yet to know.

Q. Was it a happy crew?

A. It is very difficult for a group of people to live together in a confined space for a prolonged period of time without a certain amount of friction. We had friction on board but it was never allowed to get out of hand. We would minimise the problems, perhaps sit down and argue them out and come to a compromise conclusion. Anyway, differences of opinion are good in as much as they ward off boredom. I was never bored at any time. There rarely seemed to be enough time to do everything and when I could relax I read books.

Q. What does the future hold in store for you?

A. What I want and what the Army has in store for me might be two different things. I would very much like to continue sailing and to undertake similar projects to the Round-the-World Race. The problem is that to sail on any other boat than *Great Britain II* will be a disappointment. Before we set out and all during the trip it was drummed into us that there was a danger that we would become very dissatisfied with the mundane routine of ordinary life. Although I know the dangers I am beginning to feel it already. I am becoming restless and not content with my lot. I need new challenges now. I think the Services are involved with my immediate future because of the security, but I am certainly on the look out for another opportunity.

Q. If you were to start again tomorrow with the same boat and the same crew, would you achieve more honours?

A. Without doubt. We had the advantage of being paras when we started from Portsmouth. Now we are paras who can sail as well as any crew in the world. Next time we would win Line Honours, Handicap Prize, whatever you care to name.

Q. Was the training in Scotland valuable?

A. Certainly. It taught us how to live with each other and that was a most important lesson.

Q. What was your relationship with the other crews?

A. Excellent. After the initial wariness we all became great friends and I will be keeping in touch with many of the other crew members. Of course they had their internal problems and we heard stories about French crews refusing to come on deck, and Italians having an average of one row per hour. We did not have these troubles because of our training and self-discipline.

Q. What did you think of Chay as a skipper?

A. Someone asked me on the day we came back whether we could have done as well with another skipper. I replied "No". Chay has got a quality that gets things done and sees things carried through. It is a magic quality and although I may have a number of arguments with him, I would sail with him anytime anywhere.

JOHN RIST

Q. Would you do it again?

A. I don't think so, not now that I have done it once. The race is too long to contemplate doing twice. But I would certainly like to continue sailing and racing. The Cape—Rio race or the Transatlantic would be ideal.

Q. What was the most disappointing aspect of the race?

A. Not coming in first at Cape Town. After all the sacrifices to weight we had made it was a shattering blow to see two other boats there before us. But it was just one of those things.

Q. With the experience the crew has now, could you win the Handicap Prize?

A. No way. We were penalised too heavily. Anyway, we went for Line Honours and Elapsed Time and that is what we won. Maybe if we had had a few more crew on board we could have improved our performance slightly.

Q. What was the most exciting part of the trip?

A. When we nearly hit the submerged rocks off New Zealand. It was quite a hairy experience. We did not have a large enough chart of the area and so we nearly hit the rocks. It was exciting because we missed them, but it could so easily have been tragic.

Q. Were you ever frightened?

A. Yes, a couple of times. When we broached and when we capsized with the spinnaker up. But I never thought for a moment that we would not pull through. *Great Britain II* is a very strong boat and I never had any doubts about her

Q. What about your future?

A. It is very much an unknown quantity as far as I am concerned. I have put in for a commission and I hope to get it. If so I will stay in the Army, if not who knows? I think I want to stay in the Army because I am worried about becoming bored. After this trip I could not stand a nine-to-five job.

Q. What did you think of Chay as a skipper?

A. Great. He could blow in my ear and I would follow him anywhere.

ALEC HONEY

Q. Would you do it again?

A. Yes, most certainly. I enjoyed it.

Q. Which was the most exciting part?

A. That's difficult. Certainly the most impressive part

was the start from Portsmouth. Hundreds of boats crammed together to see us off. It was very dangerous and most exhilarating.

Q. What does the future hold for you?

A. My immediate future is with the Army. I have done ten years and plan to do at least another six. I would like to continue sailing but I realise that the sort of level that we have achieved on this trip has been the highest and that I will have to be satisfied with continuing my sea-going activities in smaller craft. The important thing is to realise that I am going back to an ordinary life with a long-term future.

Q. Were you ever frightened?

A. Yes, I was frightened, particularly at the start of the trip. It is fear of the unknown that gets you. The first gale we experienced scared me, and I was also frightened when we hit really bad seas on the second leg. But I do not think I was ever panicky and as the voyage progressed so my confidence in the yacht and her crew increased. The same things would not frighten me again.

Q. Which other competitor impressed you most?

A. *Sayula.* The appearance of the boat was at all times immaculate and they were a very professional and happy crew. Ramon Carlin kept them sailing well and they deserved to win the Handicap Prize. However, it is rather unfair to single out one yacht because the fact that they were in the race is impressive in itself, and one cannot fail to admire an entrant who has sailed around the world and completed the course.

ROBBIE ROBERTSON

Q. Would you do it again?

A. Yes, I think so, but it is too soon after the finish of this race to say with any certainty. If I did do it, I would want to be in the same boat with the same crew. We are so experienced now that if we set off tomorrow we would win every prize in sight including the Handicap Prize. Let me give you an example. When we put a reef in the main on the first leg it took half-an-hour. When we did the same job on the last leg it took seven minutes.

Q. Which port impressed you most?

A. Sydney. I thrive on the sun and the beaches and the people were fabulous. I enjoyed the night life there too.

Q. Were you ever frightened?

A. When we were approaching Australia we had a real blow one night. I had just taken over the helm from Len. The wind was up to about 40 knots but both Len and I thought it was just a squall. Chay asked if I wanted a reef in the main to help ease the helm but I said no, it was only a squall and it would pass. We were really moving and I did not want to slow progress. Next thing she was picked up on this massive wave and she went faster than I had ever experienced before. She was literally flying along. The plumes of water were coming so high that they were hitting the mainsail. The weight of the water broke the preventer, and broke the boom vang. We had 60 knots of wind and I must admit my knees were shaking. I was alone and we were going faster and faster and faster. Eventually things calmed down a bit and I realised that if *Great Britain II* could come through that she could tackle anything.

Q. What was the most enjoyable part of the trip?

A. Trade Wind sailing without doubt. The wind is exactly the same all the time. The weather is glorious. You just set the sails and you will be on the same tack for a couple of days. Fabulous.

Q. What will you be doing in the future?

A. Nothing is definite but I may go over to Australia. I think it is a great country. I will make enquiries but there are so many things to consider that I could equally stay in the Army. I have been in twelve years now and if I left I would lose a good job with plenty of variety, as well as a pension. You see, the Army is not like an ordinary job. In the course of a year you might see three or four countries. What civvy job offers that? It's important. Whatever happens though, I want to carry on sailing.

PETE BATES

Q. Would you do it again?

A. I think so, but I am not as keen as some of the other members of the crew. I think the real answer is that I would go if I was paid to, but I would not undertake such a long trip just for the love of it.

Q. Was it like you expected?

A. I never thought it would be so extreme. I had not expected it to be so cold, or the waves to be so big.

Q. Were you ever frightened?

A. Definitely. When we were approaching Australia, one evening just after tea, Robbie was on the helm and suddenly the boat started to fly. It was speed like I had never known before and you could hear the wind increasing to screaming pitch. The yacht was yawing from port to starboard. Suddenly there were two almighty big bangs on deck and I really thought our day had come. The boom had been ripped from the deck. I shot through the hatchway to help. It was really hairy.

Q. What was the most enjoyable part of the trip?

A. Coming first across the finishing line.

Q. What are your plans for the future?

A. I have three or four different ideas which are constantly turning over in my mind. I have been offered a diving job in Antarctica with the British Geological Society which sounds very interesting; there is an expedition to Patagonia which appeals to me; there's the Special Air Service; or I might decide to carry on with my Unit.

Q. Now that you know the yacht and the skipper and the crew, would you make any alterations?

A. Chay is a very good skipper. I would follow him anywhere. The crew are the finest bunch of men I have ever met. The yacht is a great yacht. The only improvements I would make would be minor things. I must confess solely for crew comfort.

ERIC BLUNN

Q. Would you do it again?

A. Yes, but not immediately. If the opportunity arose in maybe a couple of years then I would do it.

Q. Was it like you thought it was going to be?

A. It was as good as I thought it was going to be, but not as bad. The skipper had experienced really bad seas in the Southern Ocean on his solo voyage and he had painted a pretty black picture of the area. In fact the leg between Cape Town and Sydney was the worst.

Q. Did you experience fear at any time?

A. When we left Cape Town we hit a gale on the nose. Until then we had not had any really bad weather and because I was not a yachtsman I did not know the capabilities of a yacht. We were heeled over at a terrifying angle going into the gale and for three days I did not sleep. I dozed, but that was all. I kept thinking that if anything happened I would be trapped down below. After the gale had subsided I knew what the yacht could stand up to and I was happier. I was frightened again when we broached in the Tasman Sea. I was at the wheel and the spinnaker went over to the port side and all of a sudden *Great Britain II* went over on her side. In less than two seconds she was over. The spinnaker blew and then she popped right up again. I was really scared that night. I was frightened for myself and I was also frightened for Len because he fell from the starboard side to the port side and disappeared into the water. Thank God when the boat righted itself he was still hanging on.

Q. Which part of the trip was the most enjoyable for you?

A. Learning how to sail. That's what I really enjoyed. Of course the ports were great too, but because we are in the Army we are used to seeing different countries. I was particularly impressed with Australia. I saw some relatives out there I had never met before and generally the people could not do enough for us. We met lots of chaps who were ex-paras—there are people from the Brigade all over the world—the weather was fabulous, and we had a great time there. When I have served my time in the Army I might well go and settle out there. I am a qualified plumber and it is one of the top trades in Australia and I know I could make a better wage out there than in England. Mind you, I might not leave the Army at all, I might sign on again because I could not stand the routine of civvy street.

ALAN TOONE

Q. Would you do it again?

A. Most definitely. I intend to continue sailing for the rest of my life, either full or part time. I have a couple of crewing jobs lined up already and I hope to build my own boat in the not too distant future.

Q. Was it like you expected?

A. No, it was not as hard as I had anticipated and the seas were not as fearful as I expected. That's not to say I was not frightened. On a couple of occasions when we broached I was too excited to worry about being afraid. The only time I was frightened and had time to think about it at that moment was when we started to leak quite badly. I was pumping out for about an hour and a half one morning, and at the end of that time the water was still coming in faster than I was pumping it out. It was about ten days before the Horn and I knew if we had sunk there we would not have stood a chance. It was a fear that there was nothing we could do about the situation. If the water was coming in faster than I could pump it out we were going to go down. I did not mention it to anyone else because really there was nothing they could do to help. Only one man could pump at a time and I had never worked harder in my life. Eventually the water started to go down.

Q. What was the most enjoyable part of the voyage?

A. There are two types of enjoyment. When we were sailing in the Trade Winds that was enjoyable because the yacht was moving beautifully and we were relaxing and sunbathing. Then, after Cape Town, we hit the really big seas and that was enjoyable because it was exhilarating.

Q. Which was the best port?

A. They all had their good and their bad points. For me, Rio was the most pleasurable even though it was very expensive. There were no problems of colour and, maybe because it was Carnival, the people seemed to be permanently happy. You could walk along the street and listen to samba bands or watch demonstrations of an ancient form of judo they practise out there.

Q. Were you ever bored or fed up?

A. I was never bored. There were a few times when I was fed up because it is a pretty gutty job in the galley. But the depressions never lasted more than half an hour.

Q. Did the crew ever complain about the food you served?

A. All the time. It didn't bother me. I suppose I served a couple of really poor meals during the whole trip but it depends what standards you are working to. I reckon considering the conditions you would not have got better meals anywhere else—but then you might not have got worse.

Q. What was a typical day's menu?

A. It depends on whether we are at the beginning or the end of a leg. Let's consider the first twenty days. Breakfast would be fruit juice and Alpen, then bacon and eggs, sausage and beans and maybe tomatoes. Lunch would be fairly light, something like soup and bread or just fruit. Evening meal was fairly substantial. We would start with a drink. Then we would have something like steak pie or meat curry—we had a lot of curry—with potatoes, peas, carrots, and perhaps rice. Sweet would be fruit salad, or raspberries and cream, something like that. It was up to me to decide the menu. I worked out the calorie and vitamin intake needed and made sure they got it each day. It is not as difficult as it sounds. The days of things like scurvy are over as long as you are served a balanced diet. Tinned foods are good substitutes for fresh foods and of course they will keep. I used to watch the chaps and vary the diet according to their needs. For instance if they began to get spotty I would increase their vitamin intake. I rationed the

Ribena and the Lucozade so that it made a difference when they had it. Some of the crew needed more feeding than others. Pete is a big lad and he eats like the proverbial horse. On the other hand Len eats very little but he does like things such as cheese and so that gives him the right sort of food intake.

Q. You were also the medic on the voyage. Did that pose many problems?

A. I am not a fully qualified medic by any means, but I have always believed that with medic work it is important to do something quickly even though, in the long run, it may turn out to be a wrong thing. There are many armchair medics who are qualified but too frightened to put their knowledge into practice. I was afraid of three things that might have happened on the voyage. One was a fractured skull, which could easily happen from a careless slip; the others were appendicitis or a broken femur. I could have coped with most other things. If either of them had occurred I would not have worried about them because you can only do what you believe from your knowledge is best. The only major case for treatment was Eddie Hope's arm. Even that was not what I call a real problem because no matter how much pain he had, even if his arm had dropped off, he was not going to die and I could only do my best until he was able to be properly treated.

I will not comment on the individuals who made up the crew of *Great Britain II*. For one thing they were all good guys and the words I chose to describe them would be lyrically monotonous. For another, paratroopers would not thank me for back-slapping. I will simply say that I could not have had a better crew, given the time and the conditions we had to choose them. They lived up to my expectations and then beyond, they gave everything to the project.

I like to think too that they have taken something away with them. We knew before the voyage began that the experience would change us all and I believe this has proved to be the case, but with every man it has proved to be a change for the better. Everyone has been affected differently but there are some changes that were universal. We are more tolerant now and more understanding of others. We realise the value of teamwork and the dangers of breaking the rules. We have seen places and met people beyond the ken of most men. We have shared confidences and learned to live with each other. We have sailed around the world together and we know the companionship of joint achievements.

The future dangers for the crew are obvious and I have taken care to point them out to each man. Ocean racing is a glamorous life and the taste we have had of it leaves many with the craving for more. I cannot believe that we will never sail together again, but there are those among the crew who will try to make sailing their life. I have spelled out the pitfalls and it may be that life ashore and the frustrations that are bound to hinder such ambitions will deter them. On the other hand they are all determined men and it will take a lot to beat them. The future for each man is a question mark but one thing is certain—there were men on board *Great Britain II* whose names you will read again.

So what of the future? Have I had enough now? Will I settle down? The truthful answer to all the questions is: I don't know.

There are priorities and I must always be aware of them. I have a wife, a daughter, and two big yachts to feed and believe me that is expensive. I will continue to lecture about my experiences and I hope to write more. I also intend to continue my association with Outward Bound because I feel the organisation does an excellent job.

But now there are new challenges to be conquered and I am looking very seriously at the world of multi-hull yachts. Just how safe are they? Are they capable of taking on the world's seas and beating them? In 1975 Whitbreads will be organising a Criss-Cross Atlantic Race for multi-hulls. The route is from here to Rio, Rio to Cape

Town, Cape Town to New York, then back here, I want to be in the race and I want to win it. Then there is the solo Transatlantic Race. And in 1977 I am told there will be another Round-the-World Race.

The Awards

II

THE AWARDS

First leg—Portsmouth to Cape Town

Adventure	1st on handicap	City of Cape Town Stinkwood Trophy
Adventure		Whitbread Gold Medal
Sayula II	2nd on handicap	Cruising Association of South Africa (Silver Tray)
Sayula II		Whitbread Silver Medal
33 Export	3rd on handicap	Royal Cape Yacht Club Trophy
33 Export		Whitbread Bronze Medal
Burton Cutter	Line Honours	Cruising Association of South Africa (Silver Tray)
Burton Cutter		RNSA Dolphin Trophy
Adventure	Best Passage	Ocean Cruising Club Plaque

Second leg—Cape Town to Sydney

Sayula II	1st on handicap	City of Sydney Trophy
Sayula II		Whitbread Gold Medal
Grand Louis	2nd on Handicap	Nestlé (Australian) Trophy
Grand Louis		Whitbread Silver Medal
Kriter	3rd on handicap	Cruising Yacht Club of Australia Plaque
Kriter		Whitbread Bronze Medal

Pen Duick VI	Line Honours	Port Jackson Trophy
Pen Duick VI		RNSA Dolphin Trophy
Kriter	Best Passage	Ocean Cruising Club Plaque

Third leg—Sydney to Rio

Adventure	1st on handicap	Brazilian Ocean Racing Association Trophy
Adventure		Whitbread Gold Medal
Sayula II	2nd on handicap	Iate Clube do Rio de Janeiro Trophy
Sayula II		Whitbread Silver Medal
Kriter	3rd on handicap	Brazilian National Council of Sport Trophy
Kriter		Whitbread Silver Medal
Great Britain II	Line Honours	The Iate Clube do Rio de Janeiro Plaque
Great Britain II		RNSA Dolphin Trophy
British Soldier	Best Passage	Ocean Cruising Club Plaque

Fourth leg—Rio to Portsmouth

Adventure	1st on handicap	RORC Silver Trophy
Adventure		Whitbread Gold Medal
Great Britain II	2nd on handicap	Rod Rigging Trophy
Great Britain II		Whitbread Silver Medal
33 Export	3rd on handicap	Camper and Nicholson Trophy
33 Export		Whitbread Bronze Medal
Great Britain II	Line Honours	Henri Lloyd Trophy
Great Britain II		RNSA Dolphin Trophy
Tauranga	Best Passage	Ocean Cruising Club Plaque

Overall Awards

Sayula II	1st on handicap	Whitbread Trophy
Adventure	2nd on handicap	Royal Naval Club and Royal Albert Yacht Club Trophy
Grand Louis	3rd on handicap	Royal Thames Yacht Club 'Velsheda' Trophy
Kriter	4th on handicap	Italvela Trophy
Sayula II	1st on handicap for Legs 2 and 3	RNSA 'Roaring Forties' Trophy
Great Britain II	Line Honours	Portsmouth City Council Trophy
Great Britain II		RNSA Dolphin Trophy (Gold)
Copernicus	Outstanding Seamanship	The Lady Swaythling Trophy (on behalf of the Shipwrecked Mariners Society)
Peter von Danzig	'Best Loser'	Royal Yacht Squadron Trophy
Guia	Team award for lowest aggregate corrected time	Federazione Italiana Vela Trophy
Great Britain II Adventure British Soldier	The Duke of Edinburgh Award for Active Service Personnel	

OTAGO (Poland). Steel ketch designed H. Kujawa and built 1960. Overall 55ft. Skipper, Zdsislaw Pienkawa. H'cap 6.281 days.

KRITER (France). Skippered by Jack Cr with experienced crew. Moulded plywood ketc designed G. Auzepy-Brenneur, built 1973. 6 overall. H'cap 3.833 da

GUIA (Italy). Design, Sparkman and Stephens, wooden 45ft sloop, built 1970. Skipper, Georgio Falck. 1972 Mediterranean Ocean Racing Champion. H'cap 8.906 days.

SAYULA II (Mexico). Standard Sparkman and Stephens 64 footer, built in Finland 1973 and owned by Ramon Carlin. H'cap 4.627 days.

SECOND LIFE (Britain). Glass fibre ketch built 1972 for single-handed transatlantic race. 71ft overall. Designed Van der Staat, owned Roddy Ainslie and Brian Langmead. H'cap 8.632 days.

BRITISH SOLDIER (Britain). Formerly British Steel which Chay Blyth sailed "wrong way" round world. 59ft steel yawl crewed by Army under John Day, George Philp, Neil Carlier and James Myatt. Design Robert Clark. Built 1970. H'cap 5.635 days.

Across the line and 30,000 miles to go

By permission of the Sunday Times

GREAT BRITAIN II Sponsor "Union" Jacl Hayward, of Lundy: s Chay Blyth; crewed by Parachute Regiment. fibre ketch, 72ft overal designed Alan Gurney built 1973. H'cap scra